PROVENCE

THE COOKBOOK

"Provence is a country to which I am always returning, next week, next year, any day now, as soon as I can get on a train. Here in London it is an effort of will to believe in the existence of such a place at all."

Elizabeth David, *French Provincial Cooking*, 1960

PROVENCE
THE COOKBOOK

Recipes from the
French Mediterranean

Caroline Rimbert Craig

Interlink Books

An imprint of Interlink Publishing Group, Inc.
Northampton, Massachusetts

First published in 2019 by

INTERLINK BOOKS

An imprint of Interlink Publishing Group, Inc.
46 Crosby Street, Northampton, MA 01060
www.interlinkbooks.com

Published simultaneously in Great Britain by Kyle Books,
an imprint of Kyle Cathie Ltd., part of Octopus Publishing
Group Ltd.

Editor: Judith Hannam
Editorial assistant: Sarah Kyle
American edition editor: Leyla Moushabeck
Design: Rachel Cross
Photography: Susan Bell
Food styling: Kitty Coles
Production: Nic Jones and Gemma John

Library of Congress Cataloging-in-Publication Data available
ISBN: 978-1-62371-920-3

Printed and bound in China

10 9 8 7 6 5 4 3 2 1

To request our 48-page, full-color catalog, please call us
toll free at 1-800-238-LINK, visit our website at
www.interlinkbooks.com, or send us an e-mail at:
info@interlinkbooks.com.

contents

introduction

This is a guide to cooking the Provençal way. For people who want to recreate the flavors of the Mediterranean at home, who want to eat simply but well on a day-to-day basis, who love to cook food for special occasions and dishes that rhyme with the seasons. It's also for people who enjoy reviving old skills, such as making homemade red wine vinegar or canning tomato coulis using authentic recipes from a family that does all of this.

My French family have been working the land in Provence for hundreds of years. The values and lessons from the joys and trials of such a life have shaped the way I live, the way I feel about home, and the way I cook for others. Growing up in England, to me Provence was almost a secret place, another life. I have a grandfather, Maxime (Papé Xime), whose knowledge of the land, its biodiversity, and the medicinal value of its aromatic herbs is unparalleled. He mows the grass under his olive trees at night so as not to disturb any bees. He also makes a mean nougat at Christmas. His mother, Antoinette, sisters, Régine and Edmée, and his daughter, my mother, Françoise, are the most talented home cooks, gardeners, and foragers I have ever known. This book shares something of our lives here and the recipes I take to life away from Provence, so you can bring a bit of this magical place into your own homes and kitchens.

My maternal ancestors hail from the southern foothills of the Mont Ventoux. The sun beats hard and dry, but aromatic herbs, vines, and fruit trees prosper. My mother grew up on a fruit farm called La Cointe surrounded by pine forests, fields, and orchards, the same farm as her father, aunts, grandfather, grandmother, and great-grandparents before her. The rigours and natural ebb and flow of peasant life meant that the women in the family learned how to deal with a glut of produce, how to make something wonderful out of almost nothing, how to feed the masses, and cook with a generosity that isn't about extravagance or showing off, but instead one of spirit, taking real joy in cooking for others and celebrating the produce.

We no longer live in that great farmhouse together as an extended family, but we pitch in with each other's grape, olive, truffle, and cherry harvests, share our produce, and gather to eat signature Provençal seasonal dishes, whether made with ingredients from the market or our own potagers. Such rituals are in keeping with Provence's cultural calendar of fêtes lauding the land and its bounty: *La Fête de la Lavande* in Sault, *La Foire aux Asperges* in Mormoiron, and *La Fête de la Figue* in Caromb.

PRESERVING PROVENCE

When we move far away from our families, cooking the dishes from home is a way of feeling close to them and keeping our traditions alive. In many ways it is because I have lived away from Provence that I have come to understand what is so special about it. And though I live in Provence happily now, I don't know where life might take me next. This book contains the rituals I take with me wherever I go and the dishes I come to again and again for the simple reason that they make me feel happy. It is not a guide to running a smallholding and I have not (I hope) directed you to buy expensive imported fruit and vegetables exclusively from the Mediterranean. I cooked Provençal dishes for many years in London using Britain's beautiful fruit and vegetables, outstanding free-range meat and, frankly, world-class seafood. This book simply tells of a way of using good ingredients, wherever we may live, using recipes passed down through the generations of my family.

Not everything is in this book. It will take me a lifetime to gather every old recipe and skill: my aunt's muscat grape juice; the homemade saucisson and goat cheese my great-grandmother Antoinette used to make; but I hope these pages are enough to inject Provençal joie de vivre into kitchens, and bring simple peasant cooking out of holiday nostalgia and into your kitchen, wherever you are.

THE RECIPES

Provence is at the crossroads of civilizations. In our fields, we find fragments of Roman amphorae, roof tiles from villas long since fallen, and arrowheads from Neolithic human societies. Though its borders are drawn by politics, Provence's soul is wide open: Mediterranean, Levantine, North African. It is the fruit and vegetable garden of France. These ingredients, combined with Provence's unique identity, position, and history, have resulted in a cuisine full of heart, balance, and soul, a cuisine that showcases its people's reverence for the produce, the changing seasons, and the land. For me, of course, these are more than just recipes, they are tied to memories: when my great-aunt Tata Edmée first had twenty of us over for soupe au pistou on her terrace; the sight of my mother canning jars of apricot and plum compotes for winter; the poignant, intimate moment that a special recipe was passed down when an older member of the family decided that it was time.

My culinary education involved watching and helping the older generation of women in my family in the kitchen, seeing things transform in the pan, tasting, noticing how a recipe was adapted, more obviously according to the season or, more subtly, according to

which particularly special ingredient in a dish was in need of highlighting. Like so many of their generation, my great-aunts and great-grandmother never owned a cookbook. Their cooking was learned, instinctive, the same dishes made slightly differently each time. Some things will remain a mystery. My sisters and I have tried to get definitive instructions from my grandfather for preparing black olives and it is never the same year-on-year. We laugh whenever we open a particularly perfect batch as he never remembers how he made them.

In many ways, this book is a snapshot of how we do things at a certain time. To cook well, we must adjust and tweak according to what is good and what is nice. Is it a delicate spring vegetable, needing only a little butter or olive oil and some fresh herbs, or a gutsy late summer vegetable, capable of standing proud alongside strong aromatics like bay leaves, garlic, thyme, and rosemary? I have made suggestions for substitutions and alternatives where appropriate, but I hope that you will use this book as a guide, make the recipes your own, and put your own stamp on dishes as you cook from it.

THE PROVENÇAL TABLE

A typical family meal in Provence is not composed of one course, requiring a vast quantity of one dish per person, but rather a main course systematically preceded by one dish and followed by another, sometimes two, which balances it out. The word "course" sounds very formal and labor intensive for the average weeknight, but this is not at all the case in reality.

Whatever the season, we will nearly always begin a meal with a salad and bread. Most often—and by this I mean five days a week—a big plate of well-dressed green leaves, generally a frisée with a garlic dressing (see page 156). Other times it might be a Salade Composée (see page 122) or a variation of one from the classic trio (see pages 78–79). Next, comes the main—a simple dish of saffron rice or something more elaborate like Tata Edmée's Eggplant Gratin (page 88). After this, we eat a piece of cheese, most often goat cheese, and this with more bread and a glass of red wine. Even those who aren't drinking wine with the meal will generally sip un *petit fond* (a small glass) to accompany the cheese. The meal is then rounded off with seasonal fruit and perhaps yogurt.

This is a food ethic I try to live by wherever I am. Each seasonal chapter in this book contains a balance of the dips, drinks, and nibbles we have for apéritif before a big family gathering, the salads we sit down to eat on a daily basis, the classic main courses we come back to again and again, and the fruit- and nut-based desserts we enjoy the most.

the provençal larder

These ingredients are the building blocks of Provençal cooking and markers of deeply embedded cultural traditions. Other ingredients in dishes will not have to work as hard if care is taken with these founding elements.

OLIVE OIL

We begin with olive oil, more precisely cold-pressed organic extra virgin olive oil: it is one of the most elegant, precious things in the world, something the people of the Mediterranean have been making the same way for thousands of years. Olives are picked when ripe in winter (see page 151), brought to a mill, pressed, and the oil collected for use until the next harvest 12 months later.

Good olive oil is indispensable for dressing salads, dips, aïoli, bourride, tapenade, brandade de morue, gratin de morue… Though it is sometimes used for cooking, it should be thought of as an aromatic rather than a cooking oil, like the sprinkling of freshly torn basil leaves or a squeeze of fresh lemon juice just before serving.

Trying to purchase Provençal olive oil outside of Provence is difficult because it is a small market relative to the Spanish, Greek, and Italian giants. It is thus both a pleasure and a privilege that we continue to produce our own as a family for household use. However, being a producer does not mean it is on tap: any grower must accept the frequent years when the trees produce few olives. When our family stock is depleted, it is our chance to seek out other olive oils from the Mediterranean, to enjoy the seductive intensity of those from Tunisia, the "green" freshness in those from Greece, no doubt picked earlier in the season, or the amber fruitiness of those from Puglia. There is no universally acknowledged "right" tasting cold-pressed organic extra virgin olive oil, it simply depends on personal preference and mood.

I learned early on the difference that good olive oil makes, how precious and so very worth the money it is and that, if chosen with care, it changes everything. If you have the means to spend a little more on a bottle of wine or an organic roasting chicken, consider buying a bottle of really special olive oil for a similar price. It will last a lot longer than the wine or the chicken and every other ingredient it is paired with will benefit.

Look for olive oil from a single region or, ideally, a single farm. Read the backs of

bottles of big brands: you will often find that, though they are ostensibly marketed in the branding as "Italian," they are in reality a blend of European, and sometimes non-European, olive oils of varying quality, blended in an attempt to homogenize and thus neutralize their flavor. This misses the point somewhat. Experiment and taste different oils until you have found one that you adore. Olive oil is best used within a year of being pressed lest it become tasteless and musty, and is best stored in glass containers in cabinets, shielded from sunlight.

HERBS AND AROMATICS

Step off the train, plane, or car arriving in Provence and the heady herb-scented air of wild thyme and pine trees envelops you.

Herbs and aromatics are weaved into cooking and into life here. If my grandfather is feeling under the weather, his first instinct is to forage for the herb containing the flavonoids and alkaloids to ease his symptoms: a thyme steam inhalation to clear the sinuses, St John's wort flowers steeped in oil applied to burns, lavender oil for most skin ailments. These plants grow wild and abundantly. A short walk in the hills behind our house provides juniper berries for pot-au-feu, rosemary and thyme for roast potatoes, sage for aïgo boulido, savory to sprinkle over fresh goat cheese, and wild fennel for olive brine… the list goes on and the cultural, aromatic, culinary, and medicinal values of these plants can never be emphasized enough.

In North America, it is possible to buy, grow, or forage for every possible herb you need to cook à la Provençale. Herbes de Provence, sold around the world, are not actually from Provence; it is the common name for a dried mixture of, typically, thyme, oregano, rosemary, and savory, used for sprinkling on roast meat, fish, and vegetables. For instructions on how to dry herbs and make your own personalized mixes see page 25.

Ironically, given the ubiquitousness of herbes de Provence, dried herbs and aromatics are stored separately in Provençal kitchens to keep more control over the balance of flavors in dishes. Those most frequently used are thyme, rosemary, savory, bay leaves, oregano, juniper berries, fennel seeds, piment d'espelette and, of course, sea salt and peppercorns.

The fresh herbs predominantly used are parsley (raw in salads or cooked in stews and broths), basil (raw in salads, pounded into pistous, cooked on pizzas), sage (in broths and roasts), mint (raw in salads), and celery hearts and fronds (raw in salads).

In Provence, as in North America, fresh herbs are expensive and sold in paltry quantities in plastic packages in supermarkets, which is bothersome, since cooking with fresh herbs requires a lot, sometimes 5–7 oz (150–200 g) of parsley or basil to make dishes taste as they should. Thus, as ever, shop in farmers' markets and forage where possible and safe to do so. (Definitely identify the plant species before putting it anywhere near your plate and do not forage adjacent to agricultural fields: the chemicals some farmers use are very harmful.) Grow what you can't buy and, if you have the space, consider cultivating common herbs anyway to have ready access to larger quantities.

Savory isn't common in North American supermarkets but is delicious, a sort of cross between thyme and rosemary. Lavender, too, is an underused aromatic in the kitchen, yet there is no guarantee when buying stems from a florist that they haven't been sprayed. It is best to err on the side of caution and grow a little pot for culinary purposes.

GARLIC

Garlic is, of course, a vital component of Provençal cooking, essential for frisée salad dressings, delicious in soups and stews, celebrated in aïoli… It is enjoyed year-round, though in spring and early summer, fresh garlic can be sought out and used in its stead.

I buy heads as large as possible for the simple reason that it is tiresome to worry about peeling tiny cloves. Une *tresse d'ail*, a braid of garlic, can be hung up in the kitchen and will stay fresh for weeks stored in this way. When cooking with garlic, whether finely chopping for soups or crushing into salad dressings and dips, the cloves must first be halved and the germinating shoot in the center removed, since it tastes bitter and is not easily digested. The exception to this rule is when whole heads of garlic are baked, for example, Garlic Roast Chicken (page 53) and Anchoïade (page 70). The heads are kept intact in these instances.

All garlic cloves in this book are large (approximately ½ oz/10 g). Use double the number indicated if you only have access to smaller heads.

SALADS

Green salads, refreshing, delicious and full of vitamins and minerals, are how almost all meals begin in Provence.

The type of dressing will depend on the leaves: with sweeter salad varieties, such as Batavia, oak leaf, or butterhead lettuces, a classic vinaigrette works perfectly. Bitter varieties, such as frisée, dandelion, and escarole, require punchy dressings, such as an anchovy (see page 126) or garlic (see page 156) vinaigrette, to balance their strong flavors. The salty, piquant nature of these dressings neutralize any bitterness in the leaves and, in my estimation, these make the best salads in the world. Crunchy Little Gem, Belgium endives, and Romaine lettuces can stand up to substantial mustard dressings and are happily chopped and tossed into potato salads. Mustardy or peppery varieties, such as arugula and watercress, are complemented by sweeter dressings with honey or balsamic vinegar and benefit from the inclusion of fruit, such as sliced figs or oranges.

Allow approximately 3–3½ oz (80–100 g) salad leaves per person for a first course—a full plate of dressed green leaves. Whole heads of Batavia, oak leaf, butterhead, or escarole typically weigh 12 oz (350 g) and are thus suitable for four to five people.

To wash a head of lettuce, pull apart the leaves, remove any bad parts, then immerse in cold water. Repeat to remove any clinging grit. The leaves must then be dried thoroughly (in batches in a salad spinner or, if you do not possess one, with a clean dry dish towel) before being tossed into dressings and immediately served. If washing a salad a day or so ahead of their intended use, it is fine to keep the leaves a little moist before placing in a bag or on a linen dish towel lightly sprinkled with water, in the fridge.

THE CHICORY FAMILY

Some explanation is necessary here, since names are different in different regions. What the British call chicory is what the French and Americans call endive, and when the French use the word chicorée they could mean any number things, including a coffee substitute made from the roots of this plant that established itself in Gallic palates during the Napoleonic and World War embargoes and shortages. Before I confuse anyone further, here is a brief guide:

– **Frisée** is also known as curly endive. It can be grown year-round but is more readily available in the colder months. Frisée can be ordered online or found in farmers' markets. Their heads are larger than your typical salad and, sometimes weighing in at over two pounds, can provide more than ten portions. They keep for up to a week in the fridge owing to their substantial chewy consistency.
– **Escarole,** known as broad-leaf endive, is grown year-round but is more readily available in the colder months. Like frisée it can be ordered online or sought out in big food markets. It is slightly sweeter than frisée but retains its substantial slightly chewy properties. As with the frisée its prized center leaves are pale in color and tender, having been blanched in the field.
– **Endive** is also known as chicory or Belgian endive. These can be white or red and are found in most supermarkets: They are delicious raw in salads (see page 154), braised in white wine (see page 137) or baked on savory tarts and in quiches.
– **Radicchio** is a larger, round, Italian variety of red endive. It can be found in most grocery stores and would be a good substitute, together with some foraged dandelion leaves in spring, for frisée, or for escarole if you cannot find it but want to try the bitter leaf salads on pages 156 and 126.

OLIVES

Olives are a staple in Provence: pounded into tapenade, baked on fougasse or pissaladière, tossed into salads, simmered in stews, or enjoyed just as they are. If you are in Provence, seek out and taste black olives from Nyons, green olives cassées, and picholines (firm, green, un-pitted, and in a delicious fennel brine).

When shopping for olives, a good-quality benchmark is when they are preserved and stored with minimal ingredients: typically salt, water, oil, vinegar, and aromatics. Chemicals are unnecessary extras and, in reality, salt and a sealed container is enough to preserve olives for years. Read the ingredients on the backs of jars and packages, since this will give a better indication of their quality than their price.

For authentic Provençal flavors in dishes, purchase un-pitted green olives in brine and mild black olives à la Grecque. This doesn't mean that the olives are from Greece but that they have been prepared using the salt-cure method, which results in beautiful wrinkly, shiny black skin and a strong yet balanced flavor. My sisters and I prepare our own black olives following this method every year (see page 153). When using such olives for cooking, they can be lightly rinsed if still coated in lots of visible salt.

For tapenade, it is simpler to use pitted olives, though generally olives, both green and black, are purchased un-pitted for the subtle nutty flavor the pits impart to the flesh when baked on bread or simmered in stews. The pits are, of course, not swallowed. Warn guests that the olive pits remain if they are unused to this.

ANCHOVIES

All of the anchovies in this book are preserved anchovy fillets in olive oil, purchased in little jars and cans. There are more expensive, delicious, freshly prepared anchovies to be found in delicatessens, but for my cooking purposes and budget, salted anchovies in olive oil from supermarkets do a sterling job.

I wasn't born loving anchovies; I used to pick them off pizza. But I knew they did something magic to Delia Smith's puttanesca pasta, which my family lived on in London in the 1990s, since without, that dish was just ordinary, lacking something. They are surely one of the best savory seasonings: melted into daubes and stews, pounded and spread on roast lamb… They can elevate subtly and deeply, like fish sauce in a Thai curry, or add punch to dressings and dips. My favorite way to use anchovies is in the best dressing in the world for the best salad in the world: see Escarole on page 126.

WINE

Wine is cooked with abandon and drunk with restrained admiration in Provence. It would be traitorous of me to say anything other than the best wines in the world are from our cave cooperative, TerraVentoux, but in any event I would never cook with a wine I wouldn't drink. Keep a bottle of white and a bottle of red on standby for cooking: even just a splash can liven up lentils, stews, and sauces. Store bottles on their side to prevent the corks from drying out, letting air in and spoiling the wine.

A few recipes in this book require a lot, sometimes even a whole bottle of wine. Wine is an expensive commodity in North America, so I will say this: when watching my spending, I halve the required quantity of wine and make up the missing volume of liquid (after the wine has reduced) with stock or hot water. The dish doesn't really suffer and no one else will know any different. It is important, however, to stick to the quantities with tough game, for example the Wild Boar Civet (see page 171), since it tenderizes the meat.

Wine bag-in-boxes have waned in popularity, but I adore those we get from our cave cooperative: the vin de table AOC is excellent, good value, easy to transport, and perfect for day-to-day cooking. I sense and hope that a bag-in-box revival is on the cards. Admittedly, I probably wouldn't serve bag-in-box wine to guests outside of the family, but for home life purposes, it is perfect: decant into a carafe, chill if white or rosé, or allow to breathe at room temperature if red.

BREAD

Baguettes "tradition" accompany all our meals. They are much smaller than some French sticks sold in American supermarkets, so I hope that readers won't think me very greedy when I suggest splitting a baguette between two people for a sandwich (see pages 41 and 104).

When a baguette is more than a day old, we serve it sliced and toasted. It can also be revived in the oven if whole by sprinkling over a little water and giving a blast for a few minutes at 350°F (180°C) and eaten immediately. On the third day, if there is still a baguette left, it can be made into Tartines (see page 120), which keep for a long time, Baguette Pizzas (see page 162) or Garlic Baguette (see page 41).

When a baguette becomes too stale to slice, it is bashed or grated into breadcrumbs (or given to a neighbor's horse). These breadcrumbs, known as chapelure, are used to top gratins and Tomates Provençales (see page 74) and can be kept in jars for a few weeks or in bags in the freezer more long-term. Buying breadcrumbs is madness.

RED WINE VINEGAR

One hears a lot of emphasis from chefs and food writers on the importance of using quality olive oil in salad dressings and marinades. Rightly so, but the vinegar should be of equal standing. In Provence, the very often homemade vinegars used for vinaigrettes and marinades are exponentially more complex than the average, pasteurized supermarket offerings: sweet yet sharp, delicious as the local wines that made them.

The good news is that the best vinegar in the world is at your fingertips, since it can be made at home with the wine you love to drink (see page 200). The process is straightforward, however, if readers are looking to replicate the taste of the classic dressings and salads in this book but do not wish to make their own vinegar, the closest to ours I have found commercially outside of France is muscat, or moscatel, vinegar.

CHEESE

The French are never without cheese and Provence is no different. Dinner parties and special occasions call for a big cheese board, but the rest of the time we keep it simple and generally only pass around one cheese at the end of a meal, most frequently fresh goat cheese, Comté, or Beaufort. Buying cheese for eating is, of course, a matter of personal preference, but in cooking, Parmesan, rindless goat cheese logs, feta, and grated Emmental are most useful.

SALT COD

Salt cod, known as morue salée, was once an integral part of the Catholic diet. Dogma dictated abstinence from meat two days a week, which meant fish. All fine and well if you lived near the coast, but in the days before refrigeration, the only way inland dwellers could eat fish was if it was preserved. We all have refrigerators now and access to fresh seafood whenever it takes our fancy, but traditional salt cod dishes are still very much a part of the diet in Provence: gratin de morue, grand aïoli, brandade, accras de morue… For aïoli, it is important to use good-looking salt cod fillets since these are served whole. However, for brandade and accras de morue it is absolutely fine to buy salt cod in cheaper, smaller pieces, since these end up pounded to a paste or chopped up anyway.

FRUIT AND NUTS

Unsurprisingly, given that we are fruit farmers, my family is devoted to fruit and nuts, and consumes them seasonally from our gardens and the local market at breakfast, lunch, and dinner. Cousin Olivier always seems to be eating a nectarine. Papé Xime's breakfast has consisted of precisely six walnuts, six almonds, eight olives, a slice of bread with jam, and a bowl of black tea every day for the past fifty years.

EQUIPMENT

Assuming your kitchen is equipped with the basics, here are the extras that I most often turn to when cooking the recipes from this book.

A salad spinner

A handheld immersion blender

An extra-large cast iron Dutch oven

A pastry brush

An 11 inch (28 cm) tart or quiche pan

A dedicated omelet pan

An extra-large sauté pan with a lid

An extra-large, tall pot: for canning, and for preparing jams and coulis

A 2–2½ gallon (8–10 liter) demijohn or carboy: for making vin d'orange, marquisette, vin de noix, etc.

"Au printemps, toute herbe est bonne salade."

Provençal proverb

spring

In March, we all begin our outdoor routines, perhaps the first tentative jogs or even lido swims, as though these actions will somehow precipitate warmer weather. This is the best time to pick young dandelion leaves to toss into salads, to forage for delicate nettle tips for soups and omelets, and if you know where to look, find wild asparagus and wild garlic. In markets and grocery stores, fruit and young vegetables begin to appear, sweet as the blossom-scented air outside: fava beans, peas, strawberries, baby carrots. And when the cherries finally arrive, we know that summer is just weeks away.

You don't have to grow your own to experience the joy at the arrival of a new season's produce, and nothing embodies this more for me than the sight of my grandfather rushing off in his battered truck to buy the first asparagus that heralds spring from his favorite producer in Mazan. We often come together as a family just to eat the dishes anchored around the new season's produce, not necessarily for a birthday or religious feast: white asparagus with vinaigrette, grand aïoli… Yet, when Easter comes, I always find that it is in many ways a celebratory feast I prefer to Christmas: the menu is not prescriptive, there is less pressure, and yet cause to celebrate and spend time with loved ones. Easter Monday calls for a picnic lunch in France, too.

In our fields, the warmer weather means there is pruning to be done. The last year's growth on the vines must have been completely cut back by March at the latest ("*taille tôt, taille tard, mais taille en mars*"), the olive trees must be thinned out and the cherry trees must too be pruned to improve the quality of the fruit and make harvesting easier.

INFUSIONS AND HERBES DE PROVENCE

The purpose of drying aromatic plants is to remove their water content while preserving and concentrating the essential oils. The advantage of drying herbs and teas is the convenience of having pinches and teaspoons of them year-round.

Drying herbs and teas

To dry medium bunches of herbs and teas with small leaves, such as thyme, oregano, or rosemary, harvest the sprigs on a warm dry day after lunch. Very fine herbs, such as thyme, rosemary, and savory, should be left on stalks during the drying process. Herbs with larger leaves, such as oregano, verbena, or lime, should be picked off stalks before drying.

To air dry, place the herbs on trays. Ensure the herbs are completely free of moisture and piled loosely. Store the trays in a dry, warm, dark place for a few weeks.

To dry in the oven, preheat to its lowest temperature. Place the herbs in a single layer on baking pans. Place the pans in the oven and dry the herbs for 1–6 hours, depending on the variety and thickness of the leaves. Open the door every so often to allow moisture to escape.

A third option available for drying broad-leaf aromatics, such as bay or sage leaves, is to tie them in bunches or hang branches upside down in a dark place. Once dried, they can be stored as they are in kitchens and pantries, or leaves picked off and kept in pots and jars in cupboards to preserve their colors. The herbs are ready to be stored once the leaves crumble when crushed between fingers. To harvest leaves dried on sprigs, rub the sprigs between your hands over a bowl wearing rubber gloves. Sieve and remove any fine stalks, then store the herbs in pinch pots, jars, or freezer bags.

If you grow aromatic herbs on a large scale, harvest the herb, stalks and all, on a hot, dry day and lay on an old linen bedsheet somewhere warm and dry for a day or two to ensure the herbs are completely free of moisture, then pick up the bundle and leave somewhere out of the way for a month. After this time, the leaves will be dry enough to fall off the woody stalks with a little encouragement by rubbing and rolling the sprigs between gloved hands. Then sieve and store.

Lavender

The bedsheet technique is also how one would dry a middling quantity of lavender. Chop on a dry summer's day with pruners, stalks included, right down to the leaves (this stops the plant from growing too spindly and woody the following year). Leave the sheet open somewhere warm at first, then pick up the bundle and leave somewhere out of the way for several weeks to dry. This process will fill your home with an incredible scent. After about a month, the flowers will be ready to pick off by rubbing and rolling the stalks between your hands. Then store.

Herb mixes

Once you have dried various herbs, you can create little jars of herb mixes according to your cooking requirements, for example, for a classic herbes de Provence mix, crush 2 bay leaves, 4 tablespoons thyme, 1 tablespoon oregano, 2 tablespoons savory, and 1 tablespoon rosemary together with a mortar and pestle (remove the stringy central part of each bay leaf). Salt and herb mixes are also handy for sprinkling over pasta or eggs on toast: if you own a spare salt or pepper grinder, fill it with a mixture of sea salt and the dried herbs of your choosing (mix the salt and the herbs together first in a bowl so that they are evenly distributed in the grinder and so the quantities and proportions can be visually adjusted at this stage).

oeufs mimosa

Oeufs mimosa are so called because once decorated with their cooked and grated yolks, they resemble the beautifully scented winter and early spring mimosa tree blossom. Here the endive leaves are used as scoops to pick up the eggs, which makes this appetizer a practical canapé as well. My cousins and I used to make platters of oeufs mimosa on Christmas Eve.

Serves 4

6 eggs

5 oz (140 g) can of tuna

3 tablespoons mayonnaise

2 teaspoons capers

1 endive

salt and freshly ground black pepper

Place a pan of water over high heat and bring to a boil, then add the eggs. Cook for 9 minutes, until just hard-boiled, then drain and set aside until cool enough to handle.

Drain the tuna into a bowl and mix in the mayonnaise and capers. Peel, then slice the eggs in half and carefully scoop out the cooked yolks. Finely grate just over half of the yolks into the bowl of tuna and mix well. Add salt and freshly ground black pepper to taste.

Finely grate the remaining yolks into a separate bowl and set aside. Picking up the hollowed eggs one by one, fill each with a heaped teaspoon of the tuna mixture, followed by a generous sprinkling of the grated egg yolks. Lay on a serving platter and repeat the steps until you have filled and garnished all of the eggs.

Pull off 12 of the largest, prettiest endive leaves and lay them on the serving platter in between the eggs. Keep the dish in the fridge until you are ready to serve.

salade de fèves et d'asperges

fresh fava bean and asparagus salad

My sister Estelle plants her fava beans on New Year's Day, straight into the ground outside. Five months later, when the sun is shining and we are eating delicious home-grown fava beans in salads such as this one, I'm very glad that someone took the trouble to sow them back in cold, dark January. If you prefer, you can serve this recipe with poached rather than boiled eggs.

Serves 2

10½ oz (300 g) podded and peeled fava beans (fresh or frozen)

1 lb 2 oz (500 g) green asparagus tips

2 eggs

¼ cup (⅓ oz/10 g) finely chopped mint, plus a few leaves to garnish

¼ cup (⅓ oz/10 g) finely chopped basil, plus a few leaves to garnish

3 tablespoons walnut oil

½ lemon

⅓ cup (1½ oz/40 g) crumbled soft goat cheese (optional)

salt and freshly ground black pepper

Place a pan of water over high heat and bring to a boil. Add the fava beans and fast-simmer for about 5 minutes. Taste one to check they are tender, and if satisfied, then lift the rest of the fava beans out of the water using a slotted spoon and place in a colander. Run the beans under cold water, then squeeze them out of their skins (unless using baby fava beans, which can be eaten whole). Place the fava beans in a salad bowl.

Trim the asparagus tips if necessary, then place in the pan of still fast-simmering water. Cook for about 5 minutes, or until tender to your liking. Lift the asparagus from the water using a slotted spoon and add to the bowl of cooked, peeled fava beans.

Place the eggs in the same pan of boiling water and set a timer for 6½ minutes, for a firm white and soft yolk (alternatively, you can poach the eggs). While the eggs are cooking, add the mint and basil to the bowl of asparagus and fava beans. Drizzle over the walnut oil, crumble in the goat cheese (if using), and add a squeeze of lemon juice. Toss together, then add salt and black pepper to taste, along with a little zest from the lemon.

Divide the salad between two plates. When the eggs are done, peel them and top each salad with an egg. Garnish as desired and serve immediately with plenty of crusty bread.

salade de pois chiches

chickpea salad

On my kitchen counter there is generally a bowl of soaking chickpeas for making salads such as this one for lunch boxes, Poichichade (page 161), hummus, or tagines. As a general rule, you should yield roughly double the original weight of dried chickpeas once they are cooked: a 2½ cup (1 lb 2 oz/500 g) package of dried chickpeas thus yields about the same quantity as four standard 14 oz (400 g) cans once drained. I know which I would rather lug home from the store.

Serves 3–4

scant 1½ cups (10 oz/275 g) dried chickpeas, (or 2 x 14 oz/400 g cans of chickpeas, drained)

½ garlic clove, crushed

2 teaspoons red wine vinegar

½ small fennel bulb, trimmed and finely sliced

1 sweet green pepper (preferably the long variety), cored, deseeded, and cut into chunks

4 inch (10 cm) piece of English cucumber, washed, deseeded, and cubed

3½ oz (100 g) radishes, sliced into rounds (generous 1 cup slices)

¼ cup (⅓ oz/10 g) chopped mint

½ cup (¾ oz/20 g) chopped cilantro

3 oz (80 g) feta

2 tablespoons olive oil

2 tablespoons walnut oil

1 teaspoon freshly ground black pepper

½ lemon

salt

If using dried chickpeas, soak them overnight in cold water, then fast-simmer them in plenty of fresh water for about 40 minutes, or until tender. Drain and cool.

Place the crushed garlic into a large salad bowl and cover with the vinegar. Follow with the drained chickpeas and the fennel. Follow with the green pepper and cucumber.

Add the radishes, followed by the mint and cilantro. Crumble in the feta, add the oils, black pepper, and a good squeeze of lemon juice. Mix, then taste to check the seasoning, adding salt as required. Serve and enjoy.

soupe de petit épeautre

small spelt soup

After the heavy soups and stews of winter, there is a lightness to this broth that heralds the warmer days to come. Having said that, if you are in possession of a leftover bone with a bit of meat on it, such as from a leg of lamb, all the better: add the bone to the pan with the soaked einkorn (small spelt) and cover with 7½ cups (1.75 liters) of water and a generous sprinkling of salt in lieu of the chicken stock. Simmer for longer than is indicated below, to draw the flavor from the bone. The leftover meat will come off with a little encouragement before you dish it out and serve.

Serves 4–6

½ cup (3½ oz/100 g) einkorn wheat berries (small spelt; or use spelt or pearl barley)

1½ tablespoons (¾ oz/20 g) butter

1 large onion, finely chopped

1 large leek, sliced into ½ in (1 cm) rounds

1 celery stick, diced

1 Parmesan rind

1 bay leaf

7½ cups (1.75 liters) chicken stock

1¼ cups (7 oz/200 g) podded baby fava beans (fresh or frozen)

handful of basil leaves, torn

2 tablespoons olive oil

salt and freshly ground black pepper

Rinse the einkorn and place in a bowl of tepid water to briefly soak while you prepare and cook the vegetables.

Place the butter in a Dutch oven or heavy-bottomed soup pot over medium–low heat. Add the chopped onion, leek, celery, Parmesan rind, and bay leaf. Sprinkle in the black pepper and gently cook for 15–20 minutes, stirring frequently and putting a lid on between stirring, until the vegetables have completely softened.

At this stage, raise the heat and add the stock. Drain and add the einkorn. Bring the broth to a boil, then lower the heat. Simmer, partially covered, for 45–60 minutes, until the grains are cooked, then add the baby fava beans. Cook for a further few minutes, then taste to check the seasoning, adding salt and black pepper if necessary. Finally, ladle into soup bowls, topping each portion with torn basil leaves and a light drizzle of olive oil.

aigo boulido

Very simple, very soothing. The name means "boiled water" in Provençal. Some prefer to simmer a chopped potato rather than pasta for this restorative, herby broth. To each their own.

Serves 1

1 sprig of thyme

3 sage leaves

big pinch of salt

1 garlic clove, crushed

scant ½ cup (2½ oz/70 g) orzo

big pinch of black pepper

butter or olive oil

1–2 tablespoons grated
Parmesan or Emmental

Place 2½ cups (600 ml) of water in a pot and add the thyme, sage, salt, and garlic. Bring to a boil, then add the orzo. Continue boiling until the pasta is fully cooked, as per package instructions.

Pour the soup into a bowl and season with the black pepper. Finish with a pat of butter or a drizzle of olive oil, and plenty of grated cheese. Enjoy.

potato salad

This salad is delicious hot or cold and is a course in itself rather than an accompaniment.

Serves 4

2¼ lb (1 kg) waxy new potatoes

2 teaspoons red wine vinegar

3 tablespoons olive oil

1 tablespoon Dijon mustard

1½ cups (6½ oz/180 g) thinly sliced radishes

10 cornichons, sliced into thin rounds

3½ oz (100 g) sweet white onions or scallions, finely chopped

sprig of dill, to serve

salt and freshly ground black pepper

Halve any larger potatoes so they are all about evenly sized, then place in a saucepan of cold water. Add salt and bring to a boil. Cook for 15 minutes, or until the potatoes are tender, then drain and set aside.

While the potatoes are cooking, prepare the dressing in a salad bowl. Begin by dissolving a big pinch of salt in the vinegar, then whisk in a pinch of black pepper, followed by the olive oil and mustard.

Add the radishes, cornichons, and onions to the bowl, along with the drained potatoes. Toss together and taste to check the seasoning. When ready to serve, use scissors to snip over some dill. Enjoy warm or cold.

white asparagus and vinaigrette

My family stopped growing asparagus in the 1980s, but our devotion to this perfect vegetable persists. Every spring, huge steaming piles of white asparagus, boiled until tender, are laid on platters lined with linen dish towels and placed on the dining table. We will each prepare our own vinaigrette in a little ramekin and once everyone has been served asparagus, we eat with our fingers, dunking spears into the vinaigrette in between bites and discussing whether tomorrow is too soon to do this all over again.

The asparagus we use is from a well-signposted farm on the outskirts of Mazan and it is truly the best reason to visit Provence in April. To cultivate white asparagus, the spears are kept covered to block out sunlight, preventing photosynthesis and keeping them sweet (lack of light is why the paler, middle parts of lettuces and celery are always sweeter too). If you wish, you can use green asparagus for this recipe—there will be no need to peel them, simply snap off the woody ends and cook for less than half of the time indicated here. The result will be different but still delicious.

Serves 6

4½ lb (2 kg) white asparagus, washed

To serve (on the table)

red wine vinegar

olive oil

Dijon mustard

salt

freshly ground black pepper

Cut up to ¾ inch (2 cm) off the ends of the asparagus and discard. Next, peel the fibrous skin around the stalks from the base to two-thirds of the way up.

Half-fill a large pan with water and bring to a boil. Lower in the asparagus. Reduce the heat to a fast simmer and cook for about 30 minutes, until the spears are completely tender from base to tip.

Line a large serving platter with a linen tea towel. Using two spatulas, carefully lift the asparagus out of the pan in batches, allowing the water to run off, and then place on the prepared platter. Owing to their size, white asparagus will keep warm for a while.

The table should now be set with plates, ramekins, and vinaigrette ingredients. Bring the platter of asparagus to the table and allow people to help themselves.

As a rough guide, here are the proportions for the vinaigrette I would typically make in my ramekin: 2 teaspoons of red wine vinegar, a pinch of salt, 2 pinches of black pepper, 2–3 tablespoons of olive oil, and a heaped teaspoon of Dijon mustard, all mixed together well.

tarte de blettes

chard tart

The town of Nice has given us more than just salade Niçoise. This tart, inspired by the classic local recipe for tourte de blettes, is reminiscent of medieval pies, with its unconventional ingredient combination by modern palate standards. Though here we keep the apples from the traditional tourte, this tart sits firmly in the savory camp.

I have the food writer and cook Sophie Missing to thank for this delicious pastry recipe. It is blind-baked in two stages, which ensures the bottom stays crisp when the wet filling goes on top. Quiches and savory tarts can be prepared in advance and served at room temperature: useful when hosting and serving multiple courses.

Serves 8,
as a first course, or 4 as a main course with a salad

For the pastry

generous 2 cups (9½ oz/270 g) all-purpose flour, plus extra for dusting

good pinch of salt

9½ tablespoons (4¾ oz/ 135 g) cold butter, plus extra for greasing

3–4 tablespoons cold water

1 egg, beaten for brushing

Cont'd overleaf.

Begin with the pastry: add the flour and salt to a bowl and whisk together. Chop the butter into cubes and rub it into the flour with your fingertips. When it has a breadcrumb-like texture, mix in the first tablespoon of water. Keep adding the water, a tablespoon at a time (four in total usually suffice), mixing and squeezing the mixture with your hands until the pastry comes together into a ball. Wrap in plastic and chill in the fridge for 30 minutes while you make the filling.

Trim and wash the chard. Use a knife to separate the green tops from their pale stalks. Roughly chop the stalks into 1½ inch (4 cm) chunks. Shred the greens, setting aside a large handful for the topping. Trim and wash the leek, then slice it into ¾ inch (2 cm) rounds.

Place a deep frying pan over medium heat and add the olive oil, chard stalks, and leek. Sprinkle with salt and black pepper and then cook, stirring frequently, for about 5 minutes. Place a lid on the pan and cook for a further few minutes while you peel, core, and roughly chop the apple into ¾ inch (2 cm) chunks. Stir the apple pieces into the pan and put the lid back on.

After another 5 to 10 minutes, add all but the reserved handful of shredded greens and place the lid on to steam. If your pan is too small, add the greens in two batches: add a first load, then place the lid on the pan. Once they have wilted and made space, add the second batch and repeat the steaming process. Remove the lid once the greens have wilted and keep stirring. When all the vegetables are silky and tender, turn the heat off.

For the filling

2¼ lb (1 kg) chard

1 leek

3 tablespoons olive oil, plus extra for drizzling

1 large sweet apple

4 eggs

3 sage leaves, finely chopped

2 sprigs of rosemary, leaves finely chopped

generous ¾ cup (200 ml) crème fraîche

1 teaspoon Dijon mustard

6½ oz (180 g) goat cheese, crumbled or sliced

salt and freshly ground black pepper

After the pastry has chilled for at least 30 minutes, preheat the oven to 400°F (200°C) and thoroughly grease an 11 inch (28 cm) quiche pan with butter and line the base with parchment paper. Remove the pastry from the fridge and roll into a circle on a piece of parchment paper lightly sprinkled with flour. Continue rolling to enlarge the circle until the dough is just ⅛ inch (3 mm) thick, and wide enough to cover the pan and then some. Lightly flour your rolling pin and the dough if necessary as you do this to prevent it from sticking.

Pick up the pastry, parchment paper and all, and flip into the pan. Gently push into position, trim the excess dough, and prick the base with a fork. Place the piece of parchment paper back on top of the pastry and fill the base with pie weights. Blind-bake the pastry for 10 minutes, then remove from the oven. Remove the weights and the top piece of parchment paper, then brush the surface of the pastry with the beaten egg, reserving any leftovers. Place the dish back in the oven for 5–10 minutes, until lightly golden. You may need to rotate the dish to color the pastry evenly.

While the pastry is in the oven, crack the eggs into a mixing bowl, and add any leftover egg you used to brush the pastry. Add the chopped herbs and crème fraîche, then whisk. Season with salt and black pepper.

Once the pastry is ready, remove from the oven and spread the mustard over the base. Distribute the chard and apple filling evenly in the pastry base, then pour the egg mixture on top. Sprinkle over the raw shredded greens you set aside earlier, and finish with the goat cheese and a final extra drizzle of olive oil.

Bake for 25–30 minutes, or until the filling has set, and remove from the oven. Remove the quiche from the pan. Wait at least 30 minutes before slicing and serving.

nettle and asparagus brouillade

A brouillade is essentially scrambled eggs, though you would not have it for breakfast in France: brouillade de truffes, brouillade de cèpes, and brouillade aux asperges are classic and delicious lunch or dinner courses, served with slices of toasted bread with butter.

For this recipe, springtime nettles are wilted in butter and combined with asparagus and eggs to make a homey yet elegant first course for six. Wear gloves when picking nettles, and choose the younger, smaller leaves from the tops of the plants. The cooking process removes any stinginess and brings out their lovely flavor, akin to spinach. If you can't find nettles, you can substitute baby spinach in this recipe.

Serves 6,

as a first course

2¼ lb (1 kg) green asparagus

2 handfuls of young nettle leaves

1½ tablespoons (¾ oz/20 g) butter, plus extra for the toast

12 eggs

6 slices of crusty bread

salt and freshly ground black pepper

First prepare the asparagus: Wash then trim the woody ends by snapping or slicing them off. Chop the spears into ¾ inch (2 cm) pieces and set the tips to one side. Bring a pan of salted water to a boil, then lower the asparagus spears in. Boil for 5 minutes, then add the tips. Cook together for a further 2 minutes, then turn the heat off, drain, and set aside.

Wearing rubber gloves, wash the nettle leaves, remove and discard any remaining bits of stalk, and finely slice the leaves. Melt the butter in a saucepan over medium heat. Add the nettle leaves and fry for a few minutes, stirring frequently, until nice and wilted.

Whisk the eggs together in a large bowl and season with plenty of salt and black pepper. Pour the eggs into the saucepan with the nettles, and follow with the cooked asparagus. Lower the heat and stir for 15 minutes, until the eggs look like they are almost cooked but still very creamy. Turn the heat off, prepare the plates, and toast and butter the bread. Stir the brouillade once more, then spoon onto the plates and serve immediately with the hot buttered toast on the side.

sandwich des cyclistes

Bicycling is France's national pastime and in spring I join my lycra-clad comrades and bike the stunning routes Provence has to offer. On the way back, as a treat for my wobbling legs, I'll pick up some bread in the village, holding it in one hand and steering with the other, for a restorative sandwich at home.

Serves 2

1 fresh baguette (about 22 in/ 56 cm long)

generous ¾ cup (200 ml) Aïoli Mayonnaise (see page 198)

4 oz (115 g) cold roast chicken

1 small ripe tomato, sliced

about 10 basil leaves

handful of wild arugula

salt and freshly ground black pepper

Cut an opening into the baguette along its length, but do not slice all the way through. Remove any excess soft dough, then spread the inside liberally with mayonnaise. Add plenty of freshly ground black pepper, at least 1 teaspoon. Slice the chicken into small pieces then add it to the sandwich. Slide in the tomato slices and sprinkle with a little salt. Finish by adding the basil leaves and wild arugula. Close the sandwich, slice in half to share with one other lucky person, and enjoy.

garlic baguette

Swap the garlic cloves and tarragon for a handful of wild garlic, if you come across some.

Serves 6

3 tablespoons finely chopped tarragon leaves

3 garlic cloves, crushed

6 tablespoons (3 oz/80 g) butter, softened

big pinch of sea salt flakes

2 big pinches of freshly ground black pepper

1 baguette (about 22 in/ 56 cm long)

Preheat the oven to 400°F (200°C).

Place the tarragon in a bowl with the garlic, softened butter, salt flakes, and black pepper. Mash and mix well.

Place the baguette on a board and slice it without cutting all the way through, so the baguette remains intact at its base. Spread 1 teaspoon of the flavored butter into each opening.

Wrap the baguette in foil with the seam at the top, then place on a baking sheet in the oven. Bake for 10–15 minutes, then remove from the oven and open up the foil. Return to the oven and bake for a final few minutes to crisp up slightly. Separate the slices with a bread knife and serve immediately.

saffron and tomato rice

This saffron and tomato rice is comforting with a luxurious edge. Delicious on its own or served alongside Garlic Roast Chicken (see page 53).

Serves 4–6

1¼ cups (9 oz/250 g) white Camargue or Arborio rice

3 tablespoons olive oil

2 onions, finely chopped

2 bay leaves

4¼ cups (1 liter) chicken stock

big pinch of saffron threads

1⅓ cups (7 oz/200 g) cherry tomatoes, halved

splash of cognac

salt and freshly ground black pepper

Rinse the rice and then soak it in tepid water for 1 hour. Drain.

Place the olive oil in a large saucepan for which you have a lid over medium heat, then add the chopped onions and bay leaves. Soften, stirring frequently, for 10 minutes.

Heat the stock until hot. Place the saffron in a little bowl and cover with a few tablespoons of boiling water to steep.

After the onions have cooked for 10 minutes and taken on a little color, add the cherry tomatoes and drained rice, followed by the cognac. Allow the alcohol to bubble away, sprinkle with plenty of black pepper, then add the stock and saffron with its water. Stir, and once the liquid is bubbling, cover the pan and lower the heat to a simmer.

Simmer, covered, for 15 minutes, until the rice has fully cooked. If there is any excess liquid in the pan, remove the lid and continue cooking to allow excess liquid to evaporate. If the rice is not yet cooked, add some boiling water and continue to cook with the lid on until it is tender. Taste to check the seasoning, adding salt if necessary, then serve immediately.

riz aux artichauts

artichokes in rice

This is how my grandmother Jacqueline loved to cook baby artichokes from her garden. Today, her son, my uncle Serge, grows them and, in springtime, generously gives us bunches and bunches every time we see him. Butter, olive oil, and lemon juice perfume this dish, but what is particularly wonderful is how the rice, cooked in the artichokes' simmering water, takes on their distinctive flavor. Omit the lardons for a vegetarian version.

Serves 4–6

8 baby artichokes

1 lemon, halved

2 tablespoons olive oil

3–4 yellow onions, finely sliced

5½ oz (150 g) unsmoked lardons

3 tablespoons (1½ oz/40 g) butter

generous 2 cups (14 oz/400 g) white Camargue or long-grain rice

salt and freshly ground black pepper

Prepare the artichokes one by one. First, remove any tough little leaves from the stem and trim the stem to a length of about 2 inches (5 cm)—this is a tender, delicious part of the plant once cooked—then peel. Next, pull off and discard the outer petals on the heads until you get to the fine, pale inner petals. Use a large knife to cut off the pointy tops of these inner petals. Halve the artichoke lengthways and use a small knife to scrape away any choke from the heart. Halve the pieces again and place in a bowl of water with a squeeze of lemon juice (save half of the lemon for seasoning the rice later). Repeat until you have prepared all the artichokes and keep them in the acidulated water while you begin to cook the onions and lardons.

Place the olive oil in a heavy-bottomed sauté pan or Dutch oven for which you have a lid over medium–low heat. Add the sliced onions and the lardons to the pan and cover. Cook for 15–20 minutes, stirring every so often, until the onions are translucent and completely cooked.

Once the onions and lardons have finished cooking, add the butter, followed by the drained artichokes, the juice of the remaining lemon half, and a few pinches of salt and black pepper. Sauté for a few minutes, stirring frequently, then cover with 3¾ cups (900 ml) of fresh water. Bring to a simmer, then cover.

Simmer the artichokes for 15 minutes, then add the rice and cook, covered, for a further 20 minutes. Make sure the heat isn't too high and check the water level after about 10 minutes, topping up with boiling water from the kettle if necessary. After 20 minutes, the rice should be cooked. If there is still liquid in the pan, remove the lid and turn the heat up a touch to evaporate. Taste to check the seasoning, adding more salt and pepper if necessary, then serve.

flageolet beans and artichoke hearts

There is a Provençal tradition for serving lamb and beans together: after a roasted leg of lamb is carved, the slices are placed on a bed of these hot flageolet beans in a stoneware serving platter. The platter is brought to the dining table where, in front of salivating guests, the host pours the hot roasting juices over the top of the sliced lamb and beans.

Beans and lamb are indeed a match made in heaven. This particular dish of flageolet beans with artichoke hearts can be served with the Daube D'Avignon (see page 54), but is also delicious alongside roast pork, or served on its own with crusty bread.

Serves 6

2 tablespoons olive oil, plus extra for drizzling

2 sage leaves

14 oz (400 g) can of artichoke hearts

4 x 14 oz (400 g) cans of flageolet beans

splash of white wine

salt and freshly ground black pepper

Place the oil in a large saucepan over medium–low heat and add the sage leaves. Fry for a few minutes while you drain the can of artichoke hearts and roughly quarter them. Drain the flageolet beans, then add them to the pan, together with the artichokes and a splash of white wine. Bring to a simmer and simmer for 8–10 minutes, then season with salt and freshly ground black pepper and a final drizzle of olive oil (unless you are pouring over roasting meat juices). Serve immediately.

brandade de morue

salt cod

Brandade de morue is as ubiquitous an appetizer nibble in Provence as hummus in the US. It is served two ways: as a canapé, spread on toasted baguette, or whipped into a hot gratin with mashed potatoes, known as brandade parmentière. The method for both can be found here.

    Brandade is happily store-bought for convenience by many a no-nonsense Provençal host such as my mother. Commercial brands are good, and it is perfectly acceptable to serve guests ready-made brandade without inducing those quietly infuriating "oh it's not homemade?" comments. Made from scratch, however, it is admittedly rather special.

Serves 8,
as an appetizer

14 oz (400 g) salt cod

1 bay leaf

⅔ cup (150 ml) olive oil, plus extra for serving

½ cup (120 ml) milk

¼ garlic clove, crushed

big pinch of freshly ground black pepper

CLASSIC BRANDADE

Start soaking the salt cod a day before you wish to serve. Rinse off any excess salt, place in a large bowl, and cover with fresh water. Soak for at least 24 hours in the fridge, changing the water at least four times. The next day, fill a saucepan with water, add the bay leaf, and bring to a boil. Lower the drained, soaked fish into the bubbling water, reduce the heat, and simmer for 10 minutes. The fish is ready when it is opaque and it flakes apart when teased. Remove using a slotted spoon and place on a chopping board. Use a fork to pull the flakes apart and check for any bones, then place the fish in a large mortar and bash to a paste.

Place three pans, two small and one medium, on the stovetop. Place the oil in one small pan, and the milk in the other. Place the mashed fish in the third, larger pan. Gently heat the oil and milk, and once warm, turn the heat to the lowest setting under the fish pan. Add 1 tablespoon of warmed olive oil to the fish pan, followed by 1 tablespoon of warm milk. Use a wooden spoon to beat the oil, milk, and fish together vigorously. (Ensure that the heat under the pan is only warming, not cooking the dish while you do this.) Once the mixture has emulsified, add another tablespoon of both milk and olive oil and beat together again. Repeat the process, adding a spoonful of olive oil and milk at a time, until a rich, creamy white paste has formed: the brandade.

Decant the brandade into a bowl. Stir in the garlic and top the bowl of brandade with black pepper and a little extra olive oil before serving on tartines (see page 120) or on freshly toasted bread for a delicious appetizer.

Serves 4,

as a main course

1 tablespoon olive oil, plus extra for drizzling

1 lb 2 oz (500 g) potatoes

splash of milk

1 quantity of classic Brandade de Morue, prepared as above

freshly ground black pepper

BRANDADE PARMENTIÈRE

Follow the method described on page 47 and chill the brandade in the fridge (it will keep for a good day or two) until 45 minutes before you would like to serve.

Grease a medium gratin or pie dish with 1 tablespoon olive oil.

Scrub and peel the potatoes. Chop them into equal-size pieces and place in a pan of fresh (unsalted!) water. Bring to a boil, then lower the heat and simmer vigorously for 15 minutes, until tender.

Preheat the broiler to high. Drain and mash the potatoes until completely smooth. Stir in a splash of milk and a pinch or two of black pepper. Beat in the prepared brandade and taste to check the seasoning, adjusting with additional black pepper, olive oil, or even salt if necessary. Spoon into the gratin dish, using a fork to create peaks on the top. Finish with a final drizzle of olive oil and a sprinkling of black pepper, then place under the broiler for 10–15 minutes, until the top is slightly golden and crisp in places.

Spoon onto warmed plates and serve immediately with hot toasted bread and Salade Frisée (see page 156) or dandelion salad.

grand aïoli

Grand aïoli, as the name implies, is for crowds: platters of seasonal vegetables, steamed or boiled, poached salt cod fillets, boiled eggs, trays of shellfish, and of course bowlfuls of aïoli made with the very best olive oil one can afford. It makes for a special gathering and can be served hot or at room temperature, as a lunch buffet.

A true aïoli is a raw garlic and 100 percent olive oil mayonnaise. It is significantly stronger tasting than "ordinary" garlic mayonnaises you may have already encountered because these and, indeed, most regular mayonnaises are predominantly composed of neutral oils such as peanut or sunflower oil.

Grand aïoli is in reality made all year round. In the spring, we use new season fresh garlic when available. In the summer, we might add green beans and zucchinis, and so forth, until Christmas Eve, when this is a traditional menu choice for many Provençal families, and the seafood platter is rendered more luxurious with the addition of cooked langoustines. As ever, you can replace the salt cod with smoked haddock and simply omit the soaking time indicated.

Serves 8

8 salt cod fillets (or smoked haddock fillets)—one per guest

3 lb 5 oz (1.5 kg) potatoes

2 fennel bulbs

1 lb 2 oz (500 g) turnips (about 8 small)

14 oz (400 g) carrots

1 cauliflower

3 leeks

4 eggs (½ egg per person)

14 oz (400 g) cooked jumbo shrimp with tails

7 oz (200 g) cooked whelks with shells (optional)

salt

For the aïoli

4 garlic cloves

4 egg yolks (at room temperature)

generous pinch of salt

3 cups (700 ml) olive oil

Soak the salt cod for 24–48 hours in a large mixing bowl of fresh water. Change the water as frequently as possible.

A few hours before serving, prepare the aïoli in two batches. To make the first batch, crush two garlic cloves into a mixing bowl. Add two egg yolks and a pinch of salt, then whisk together. Whisk in 1½ cups (350 ml) of the olive oil, one teaspoon at a time. The mixture should thicken and emulsify as each teaspoon of oil is added and form a beautiful bright yellowy-green, thick mayonnaise. Place in the fridge and make a second bowl of aïoli. If the aïoli splits at any point before serving, do not panic, and certainly do not throw it away: see page 199 for instructions for how to easily rescue it.

Once the aïoli is ready, begin cooking the vegetables. Turn the oven to the lowest setting and put in one or two large serving platters. Fill an extra-large pan with fresh water. Peel the potatoes, halving any large ones so they are all evenly sized. Wash, trim, and halve the fennel bulbs. Trim and peel the turnips. Trim the carrots but leave them whole. Add everything to the pan with a pinch of salt, bring to a boil, then lower the heat a touch and fast-simmer for 20–30 minutes, or until all the vegetables are tender.

Bring a second pan of fresh salted water to a boil. Separate the cauliflower into florets. Trim, wash, and halve the leeks widthways so they fit in the pan, then simmer both for 5–10 minutes, until tender. While cooking, poke the different vegetables and use a slotted spoon to remove any that are tender before the remainder and place on the warmed oven platters, covered with foil. Once all the vegetables have cooked, drain and arrange them on the platters, cover with foil, then place back in the warm oven while you cook the fish and eggs.

Refill both of the pans you used for boiling the vegetables with fresh water, but this time don't add salt. Bring to a boil, then lower the drained salt cod fillets into the larger of the two, and the eggs into the other. Poach the salt cod for about 10 minutes, until opaque and flaking. Boil the eggs for 9 minutes, then drain.

Drain the cooked fish in a colander. Peel off the eggshells. Halve the eggs and arrange with the salt cod on a serving platter. Place the shrimp and whelks on another. Bring all of the dishes to the table, the platters of vegetables, the bowls of aïoli... Encourage diners to help themselves to a little bit of everything.

poulet au pastis

Pastis is probably as emblematic of Provence as rosé. For readers unfamiliar with this apéritif, it is an aniseed-flavored spirit served in slim tumblers and topped with chilled water that turns it a milky color on contact. Ice cubes are added last.

In cooking, pastis can be used in fish and shrimp marinades, but in this recipe for a kind of chicken stew, it complements the aniseed notes in the fennel and tarragon. I would encourage readers to get in the habit of jointing whole chickens themselves for curries, stews, casseroles, and one-pot dishes such as this. It is better value and adds a range of meat textures to any given dish. Furthermore, you are left with a carcass with which to make a chicken stock (see page 198). Skip the jointing and buy bone-in chicken thighs and drumsticks if short on time, but bear in mind that, in this dish, no one will notice if the bird was hacked away inexpertly in a hurry.

Serves 6

3–4 tablespoons olive oil

2 lb 14 oz (1.3 kg) free-range chicken, jointed into 6 pieces

1 fennel bulb, halved, fronds set aside to garnish

3 yellow onions, sliced into ¾ inch (2 cm) thick slices

2 garlic cloves, sliced

1⅔ cups (400 ml) chicken stock (fresh or from a bouillon cube)

3 tablespoons pastis

½ oz (15 g) tarragon, leaves torn

1 lb 2 oz (500 g) green asparagus, trimmed and sliced into 2 inch (5 cm) pieces

juice of ½ lemon

salt and freshly ground black pepper

Place a large Dutch oven or pot over medium–high heat and add 3 tablespoons of the olive oil. Brown the chicken in batches, setting the pieces aside on a plate as you go.

Once this stage is complete, lower the heat and allow the pan to cool while you prepare the vegetables. Place each fennel half cut-side down on your chopping board, then slice from the base of the bulb upwards to create long pieces about ¾ inch (2 cm) thick: the fennel will fan out nicely into segments with a little encouragement.

Add the onions, fennel, and garlic to the pot and stir to coat in the chicken juices. Add a tablespoon more of olive oil, if necessary, then gently soften for 20 minutes with the lid on, stirring occasionally. While the onions, fennel, and garlic are cooking, reheat the stock, (or dissolve a bouillon cube in boiling water, if using).

After the onions and fennel have been cooking for at least 20 minutes, return the chicken to the pot and raise the heat. Pour over the pastis, allowing it to mostly bubble away for a minute or two, then add the stock, tarragon, and some black pepper.

Place a lid on the pot and lower the heat to a simmer once more. Cook for 20 minutes, stirring every so often, then add the asparagus chunks and lemon juice. Mix, then simmer for a further 15 minutes.

The chicken should fall off the bones easily once cooked through. When ready to serve, taste to check the seasoning, adding salt and more black pepper if necessary. Top with the reserved fennel fronds and bring the pot to the table.

garlic roast chicken

This is the first love-letter to garlic in this book. For the second, see the Anchoïade (page 70). Here, whole heads of garlic are halved and placed under a roasting chicken and, once cooked, are transformed into ludicrously soft and sweet little parcels, particularly if using spring's fresh garlic crop. When lifting the pan to baste the chicken, the garlic can sometimes sneak out. It is wise to tuck any back into their original position under the chicken before putting the dish back in the oven to prevent them from burning.

Serves 4–5

3 lb 5 oz (1.5 kg) whole chicken

3 large heads of garlic

½ lemon

3–4 tablespoons olive oil

1 tablespoon dried thyme

salt and freshly ground black pepper

Preheat the oven to 400°F (200°C). Place your chicken in a snug but deep roasting pan. Slice the heads of garlic in half horizontally and place one-half in the cavity, along with the lemon. Place the remaining five underneath the chicken in the roasting pan, cut-side up, so the bird is sitting on top of the garlic (you may need to trim the stalks so they sit flat on the pan). Drizzle olive oil all over the bird, followed by the thyme and plenty of salt and black pepper.

Roast in the oven for approximately 20 minutes per 1 lb (450 g), plus an extra final 15–20 minutes. Baste every 15 minutes. Oven temperatures do vary and I would recommend checking whether the juices run clear after an hour or so. Once cooked, cover the chicken with foil and clean dish towels and leave to rest while you finish any accompaniments, for example, Saffron and Tomato Rice (see page 42) and Celeriac, Carrot, and Red Onion Salad (see page 155). The bird will keep warm for a long time covered this way.

When ready to serve, reheat the juices, if necessary, and pour into a gravy jug to serve alongside the chicken. Carve the rested chicken and place on a warmed serving dish with the roasted garlic: half a head per person.

daube d'Avignon

Avignon is our nearest city, about a forty-minute drive away from our fields. For three-quarters of a century it held the seat of Western Christianity when the papacy left Rome and established itself there. Its seven consecutive residential popes left their mark, building an outstanding palace and planting vines for their own wine, most notably at what became known as Châteauneuf du Pape.

Viticulture has been practiced in Provence since the Phoenicians brought their winemaking knowledge to Marseille, or Massalia as it was called then. My great-aunt Régine found wine amphora fragments in our fields, where we suspect a large Roman Villa once stood around 400AD. Yet it was the Popes' presence in Avignon in the 14th century that brought prominence and endorsement to the region's wine, where aided by the Rhone river, trade subsequently flourished.

In medieval times, white and something akin to rosé wine were predominantly drunk here, not red. This perhaps provides something of an explanation for this old recipe for daube d'Avignon: a stew made with lamb shoulder and, somewhat unusually for red meat, white wine.

Serves 8

4½ lb (2 kg) diced lamb shoulder

For the marinade

2 onions, roughly chopped

3 garlic cloves, chopped

6 sprigs of parsley, roughly chopped

2 tablespoons olive oil, plus extra if needed

4 sprigs of thyme

4 sage leaves

2 bay leaves

1 tablespoon white wine vinegar

750 ml bottle of white wine

For later

2 tablespoons olive oil

2 carrots, chopped

salt and freshly ground black pepper

First, prepare the marinade: place the diced lamb in a large mixing bowl and add the prepared onions, garlic, and parsley, followed by the olive oil, thyme, sage and bay leaves, vinegar, and wine. Stir to coat evenly, then marinate in the fridge for at least 2 hours.

Once the lamb has marinated, preheat the oven to 320°F (160°C). Add the 2 tablespoons of olive oil to a Dutch oven or oven-safe, heavy-bottomed pot for which you have a lid, and place over medium heat. Then, using tongs, remove the chunks of lamb from the bowl of marinade and brown in batches. Set the browned meat aside in another bowl as you go, and add more oil if and when needed.

After you have finished browning the meat, lower the heat, then using a slotted spoon, strain the chopped onions, garlic, and herbs from the marinade and transfer to the pot, reserving the marinade liquid for later. Add the chopped carrots, then stir continuously for a few minutes to avoid them catching, since the pot will have retained some heat from browning the meat.

Gently cook the herbs and vegetables for 15 minutes, then return the meat to the pot. Cover with the reserved marinade liquid and add salt and black pepper. Increase the heat and allow the liquid to bubble away for a few minutes, then cover and place in the oven for 3 hours, until the lamb is tender.

Serve immediately, or cool and then reheat slowly when ready to eat. Serve with mashed potatoes, flageolet beans, or tagliatelle.

Provençal goat cheese

If you don't have time to go to a cheese shop, or your local grocery store doesn't have a strong selection, soft goat cheese logs, available in almost every supermarket, can be very easily improved and made into something that looks and tastes very special for a cheese course. All you need are a few herbs and aromatics from your pantry or garden. In Provence, it is common to add a sprinkling of salt, pepper, or savory (*la sariette)* to even the most upmarket, unpasteurized fresh goat cheese before serving.

Serves 6

2 x 5½ oz (150 g) soft rindless goat cheese logs

1 teaspoon freshly ground black pepper

½ teaspoon chopped fresh or dried thyme or oregano

½ teaspoon chopped fresh or dried savory or rosemary

pinch of lavender or other edible flowers

2 pinches of salt flakes

1–2 tablespoons olive oil

Remove the goat cheese logs from their packaging and place on a chopping board. Wait 2 minutes, then slice each log into ¾ inch (2 cm) rounds. If any rounds crumble apart, gently press back together into the desired shape.

Place the cheese on a serving plate and sprinkle with the toppings of your choosing, aiming for two of each and two left plain with just a light sprinkling of salt flakes. Finish with a drizzle of olive oil.

Allow the cheese to come to room temperature for an hour before serving with bread and red wine.

date and orange blossom madeleines

Madeleine molds are necessary to create the telltale shell shape of these lovely little sponge cakes. If you only possess one, bake these in batches, but ensure the mold is cleaned, brushed again with melted butter, and dusted with flour to prevent the subsequent batch from sticking.

Madeleines are best served hot and made to order. They only take about 9 minutes to bake and the batter can happily sit in the fridge until needed: perfection after dinner with black coffee.

Makes about 20

3 medjool dates, pitted

1 tablespoon orange blossom water

7 tablespoons (3½ oz/100 g) butter

generous ¾ cup (3½ oz/100 g) all-purpose flour, plus extra for dusting

2 eggs

½ cup (3½ oz/100 g) sugar

½ teaspoon baking powder

zest of ½ orange

confectioner's sugar, for dusting

Chop the dates into very small pieces and place in a small bowl. Cover with the orange blossom water and leave to soften while you melt the butter.

Place the butter in a pan over very low heat (if your burner is hot even on its lowest setting, melt the butter over a bain marie instead). Once completely melted, turn the heat off. Dip a pastry brush into the pan and brush the insides of the madeleine molds with a little of the butter. Sprinkle with some flour, then set the molds aside in the fridge or freezer until you are ready to bake.

While the butter cools slightly in the pan, whisk the eggs and sugar together in a bowl until pale. Next, whisk in the baking powder and orange zest, followed by the remaining melted butter. Stir in the flour and soaked dates. Place the batter in the fridge to rest for at least 1 hour, or overnight.

Thirty minutes before you are ready to serve, preheat the oven to 425°F (220°C). Once the oven is hot, remove the batter from the fridge, stir briefly to redistribute any pieces of date that may have sunk to the bottom, then add a heaped teaspoon into each of the prepared madeleine molds, ensuring they are no more than two-thirds full.

Bake for 8–10 minutes, until the cakes have risen and are lightly golden. Use a knife to coax them out of the molds. Dust with confectioner's sugar and serve immediately with coffee.

blossom honey and almond cake

My sister Estelle once spent a long day making the amaretti cookies in Patience Grey's *Honey from a Weed* from scratch. She picked wild almonds from a tree near our old Grenache vines, walked home, sat on the shaded terrace breaking the shells with a hammer, and blanched and peeled the almonds one by one. Then, following the traditional method, she pounded them to a flour using a mortar and pestle. Estelle made her little cookies with visions of these amaretti belonging in a hallowed tin for special occasions, to be savored, eyes closed, with restrained gourmandize and a cup of hot black coffee. But this was not meant to be, since someone, who to date has not confessed, scarfed the whole tin a few days later while Estelle was away.

This delicious little moist cake will take significantly less time than Estelle's amaretti. The type of honey you use will, of course, affect the final taste: I use raw set Provençal acacia blossom honey rather than clear honey, though it means harder work at the beginning when beating it into the butter. The result is really rather wonderful tasting but looks quite ordinary so I would recommend decorating the cake with lovely fresh fruit.

Serves 6–8

1 stick and 3 tablespoons (5½ oz/150 g) softened butter

scant 1 cup (5½ oz/150 g) raw set or clear blossom honey

3 eggs

1 cup (3½ oz/100 g) almond meal

6 tablespoons all-purpose flour

1 teaspoon baking powder

pinch of fine salt

heaped 1 cup (7 oz/ 200 g) sliced strawberries, for decoration (optional)

Preheat the oven to 400°F (200°C). Grease and line an 8 inch (20 cm) springform cake pan with parchment paper.

Place the butter and honey in a large mixing bowl and beat with a wooden spoon until a smooth paste has been obtained. Add the eggs and whisk together for 2 minutes. In a separate bowl, mix the almond and all-purpose flours with the baking powder and salt, then fold into the bowl of wet ingredients.

Pour the mixture into the prepared pan and bake for 20–25 minutes. After 20 minutes, skewer the center of the cake with a toothpick. If it comes out clean, the cake is ready. Wait a few minutes, then remove the cake from the pan, peel off the paper, and cool on a wire rack. Decorate with sliced fresh strawberries, if using, and serve.

cerises au soleil

sun cherries

If you have ever walked through villages in Provence in high summer, you may have glimpsed jars of cherries, sitting on tables and windowsills in the full sun. Cerises au soleil are surely one of the most romantic and simple preparations we do in Provence: cherries simply left outside, slowly preserved by the daily scorching heat, the eau de vie, and the sugar in which they sit.

Cerises au soleil make a beautiful, albeit very boozy, addition to desserts and cocktails. At home, we spoon a few into fruit salads, or top scoops of ice cream with them. At dinner parties after coffee, we serve a tray of little glasses filled with a single preserved cherry and their sun liqueur. Kept sealed, the jars can be stored for a long time. We are always finding forgotten jars of them in the dusty corners of my grandfather's garages, cupboards, and household nooks.

Serves 6–8

a few handfuls of fresh firm cherries, such as Napoléons

¼ cup (1¾ oz/50 g) sugar

small glass of 180 proof (90%) eau de vie, if available (or a large glass of 80 proof/40% fruit alcohol or vodka)

Equipment: 1 sterilized pint-size (16 oz/500 ml) jar (or 1 sterilized pint and a half/ 24 oz/700 ml jar, if using fruit alcohol or vodka)

Wash and dry the cherries and trim the stalks to a length of ½ inch (1 cm). Fill your jar three-quarters of the way with cherries.

Sprinkle over the sugar, followed by the eau de vie. If you cannot find eau de vie, a neutral 80 proof (40%) fruit alcohol or vodka will do, but you will need to double the quantity.

Cover the jar and place in the full glare of the sun for 3 months, turning over every few days to begin with, to help the sugar dissolve. When the summer is over, store in a cool place. Once opened, keep the jar in the fridge and enjoy within a few months.

gâteau aux cerises

cherry cake

Though impractical to bite into a cake and have to spit out a cherry pit, in French baking it is very common to leave them in, since they impart a wonderful flavor. For this simple cherry cake, the question of "to pit or not to pit" is left to the baker, though guests will need to be forewarned if they are indeed left in, *à la Française*.

A cherry pitter is the tool for the job if you have decided to remove them, however, if you don't wish to spend money on a niche item of sporadic use and varying effectiveness, a chopstick can be employed instead if the cherries are ripe enough. Pierce the stalk head and push the chopstick through until the pit pops out the other side.

Serves 6–8

10½ oz (300 g) cherries

2¼ cups (10 oz/275 g) all-purpose flour

pinch of salt

scant 1 cup (6 oz/175 g) sugar

2 teaspoons baking powder

7 tablespoons (3½ oz/100 g) butter

4 eggs

⅓ cup (80 ml) Kirsch (optional)

Preheat the oven to 400°F (200°C). Grease and line a deep 9 inch (23 cm) round cake pan. Rinse and dry the cherries and remove the pits if desired.

In a mixing bowl, whisk together the flour, salt, sugar, and baking powder. Place the butter in a small saucepan over low heat and melt it while you beat the eggs into the dry mixture. Pour in the melted butter and beat the mixture together. Stir in the cherries, then spoon into the prepared cake pan.

Bake for 1 hour, or until a sharp knife inserted in the center comes out clean. If the top is browning too fast, cover with foil.

Once ready, remove the cake from the pan and flip onto a wire rack to cool. At this stage, it is nice, though by no means obligatory, to pour Kirsch all over the cake while still warm. Serve at room temperature with crème fraîche, if you like.

"Il ne fait pas bon de travailler quand
la cignale chante."
Provençal proverb

summer

Stroll through any Provençal village at midday during the summer and you will almost certainly hear the clink of silverware and a murmur of voices through closed, pastel-hued shutters. Lunch is often eaten indoors and in semi-darkness, since to keep houses cool the sun must be shut out.

Dry, hot summers and their bounty of eggplants, tomatoes, onions, and peppers have resulted in iconic, gutsy Provençal dishes, such as anchoïade, ratatouille, and pissaladière, but there are others, humbler perhaps, that don't grace the menus of bistros but that home cooks turn to again and again: the gratins, the soups, the warm potato salads… The way many of these dishes work is that fresh and contrasting flavors are added at the very end, seconds before eating: enormous bunches of basil are pounded with garlic to form a pistou and spooned into bowls of vegetable soup; salt, crushed garlic, olive oil, and vinegar are drizzled over steaming just-boiled potatoes and green beans; sliced parsley, onion, and lemon juice are tossed into cooked chickpeas. It's how the fresh and sharp are paired with the sweet and cooked that really lifts and makes these dishes endure.

Summer also means visitors. Friends come to the south to stay and we will cook outdoors as much as possible to keep the house from heating up, whether on barbecues, Les Grillades (see page 102), or deep-frying nibbles such as panisses, accras de morue, and eggplants for special apéritifs. Indeed, apéritif is very much a way of life at this time of year. The drinks are important, of course—rosé, pastis, vin d'orange, and marquisette—but the nibbles that go with them are really the point of turning up on time to any dinner party here: tartines, tapenade, olives, eggplant caviar, anchoïade, etc… Santé!

artichoke dip

Jarred artichokes are delicious, but pricey. Blending them to a paste makes them go further.

Serves 4

12 oz (350 g) jar or can of artichoke hearts

½ garlic clove, crushed

½ lemon

pinch of oregano leaves

3 tablespoons crème fraîche

20 little toasts or Tartines (see page 120)

2 tablespoons extra virgin olive oil

salt and freshly ground black pepper

Drain the artichoke hearts and place in a mixing bowl. Add the crushed garlic, followed by a squeeze of lemon juice, the oregano leaves, and the crème fraîche. Blend to a rough paste using a handheld immersion blender, then sprinkle in salt and black pepper to taste. Spread on little toasts or tartines and finish the slices with a drizzle of olive oil just before serving.

Tonton Serge's caviar d'aubergines

Delicious on slices of warm toasted bread with rosé. The eggplants could be cooked on a naked flame if you own a gas stove, or straight on a wood burning barbecue when it is first lit. However black or blistered the skin becomes, it is only ready once the eggplant is soft and floppy.

Serves 8

3 lb 5 oz (1.5 kg) eggplants

2 garlic cloves, crushed

2 teaspoons ground cumin

6 tablespoons olive oil, plus extra for drizzling

2 big pinches of freshly ground black pepper

1 lemon

3–4 big pinches of salt

Preheat the oven to 400°F (200°C). Wash the eggplants and place them whole on a baking pan. Prick each a few times with a knife, then bake for 45 minutes to 1 hour, or until completely soft and floppy.

Halve the cooked eggplants and scoop out the flesh, discarding the skin and stalks. Place in a deep bowl and add the garlic, followed by the cumin, olive oil, black pepper, the juice from half of the lemon, and a little of its zest. Purée using a handheld immersion blender, then add salt gradually until you are happy with the flavor. Adjust with more lemon juice, if needed, and finish with a drizzle of olive oil and black pepper.

olive and rosemary fougasse

Many traditional Provençal recipes such as this one for fougasse, a bread enriched with olive oil, say to use *eau de source*, untreated water from a local spring. I once took joy in following such instructions to the letter, dutifully bicycling to a parcel we call Canebiers and collecting water from the source there to see if it made a difference. I cannot be sure if it did but I enjoyed the whimsy.

Like a Pompe à Huile (see page 191) or Couronne des Rois (see page 196), fougasse is one for the weekend, for the kind of day you fancy spending at home baking something. If I've been invited somewhere for supper and I have the time, I love to bring one of these for the *apéro*. Sun-dried or halved cherry tomatoes, thyme, or even cooked lardons and grated cheese make nice alternative toppings.

Serves 4

For the starter

¼ oz (7g) envelope instant yeast, or ¾ oz (20 g) fresh yeast

1 teaspoon sugar

⅓ cup (1¾ oz/50 g) white bread flour

3 tablespoons tepid water

For the fougasse

10½ oz (300 g) strong white bread flour, plus extra for dusting

½ cup (125 ml) tepid water

⅔ teaspoon salt

3 tablespoons olive oil, plus extra for drizzling

handful of unpitted green or black olives

3 sprigs of rosemary

1–2 teaspoons salt flakes

1 tablespoon oregano

First activate the yeast: mix the starter ingredients together in a bowl (crumble the fresh yeast, if using), then cover with plastic. Set aside on the counter for an hour, until the dough has increased in size and bubbles are visible on its surface. Your starter is ready.

Begin the fougasse: sift the flour into a mixing bowl, add the tepid water, the prepared starter, salt, and olive oil. Mix well, then cover and set aside for 5 minutes. Transfer the dough to a clean, dry, lightly floured surface and begin to knead. Knead for 15 minutes until a stretchy, springy dough has formed, then shape into a ball and place back in the mixing bowl. Cover the bowl with plastic and place in a warm, draft-free place to rise.

Once the dough has doubled in size, usually after 2–3 hours depending on the ambient temperature, punch down and knead once more briefly. Sprinkle flour over a baking pan and set the dough on it. Roll into an oval, ¾ inch (2 cm) thick, then slice diagonal slits in the dough in a wheat pattern. Enlarge the slits using your fingers. Cover the fougasse with plastic or a damp dish towel and set aside again to proof in a warm place for 1–2 hours. Towards the end of this time, preheat the oven to 475°F (240°C).

Remove the plastic or dish towel and lightly press olives into the surface of the dough. Pick the rosemary leaves off the sprigs and again lightly press into the dough. Sprinkle with the salt flakes, oregano, and a little drizzle of olive oil.

Bake the fougasse for 15–20 minutes. It will not get darker than a pale golden brown, but check it is cooked by tapping the base and listening for a hollow sound. Fougasse is best eaten within 2 days.

anchoïade

Anchoïade is one of those love-it-or-hate-it dishes: an intensely flavored dip thanks to the eponymous anchovies that make it. We serve it warm with crudités. This recipe comes from my grandfather's partner, Violette, and requires the biggest, most beautiful garlic heads you can find. Some purists may balk at the addition of garlic, but this is how we eat it. Though a classic *apéro* nibble, I often make this for lunch alongside a second platter of cooked ham or chicken, fresh baguette, boiled eggs, and cheese: a Provençal picnic of sorts.

Serves 8,
as an apéritif nibble

For the anchoïade

2–3 large whole heads of garlic

1¾ oz (50 g) drained anchovies (about 15)

3 tablespoons olive oil

big pinch of freshly ground black pepper

For the crudités

3 carrots

3 celery sticks

¼ cauliflower

1 white or red endive (or a mixture)

5½ oz (150 g) radishes

⅔ cup (3½ oz/100 g) cherry tomatoes (optional)

handful of salad greens (optional)

Preheat the oven to 400°F (200°C) and place the heads of garlic, as they are, on a baking pan. Place in the oven and bake for 1–1½ hours, depending on the size of the heads. To check the garlic is sufficiently cooked, pull off a clove and squeeze: the flesh should ooze out of the skins in a cream- to light brown-colored purée.

Once ready, while the heads are still warm but cool enough to handle, detach the cloves one by one and squeeze out the flesh. Place the garlic purée in a small saucepan and add the anchovies and 2 tablespoons of the olive oil. Gently heat the mixture over the lowest heat for a few minutes, stirring all the while, until the anchovies have dissolved into the garlic. If the lowest heat is still quite hot, as can sometimes be the case, lift and hover the pan above the heat while stirring: the aim is to melt, not cook, the anchovies.

Turn off the heat, then season the anchoïade with the black pepper. If serving immediately, spoon into a serving bowl and drizzle with the remaining 1 tablespoon of olive oil. If making in advance, leave in the pan and gently reheat just before serving.

Wash and arrange the crudités on a large platter. If you wish, peel the carrots and chop them into batons, along with the celery. Slice the cauliflower into little florets. Separate the endive leaves. Serve the crudités alongside the bowl of warm anchoïade. Enjoy.

tomato and blistered pepper salad

Tomatoes should be kept in the fruit bowl, never the fridge. In the bowl, they will continue to ripen and sweeten, improving their texture and flavor after a few days. This is probably the recipe I am going to feel most guilty about because you really do need excellent tomatoes, tomatoes that really taste like the fruit that they are, and these are difficult to find out of season or if you don't live somewhere hot enough.

Serves 4

2 peppers (1 red, 1 yellow)

1 lb 10½ oz (750 g) ripe tomatoes (about 3 coeur de boeuf—beefsteak tomatoes)

2 tablespoons capers

4 anchovies

¼ cup (60 ml) olive oil

2 teaspoons red wine vinegar

½ lemon

sea salt and freshly ground black pepper

Begin by cooking the peppers. Preheat the broiler to its maximum temperature. Slice the peppers in half and remove the seeds, white cores, and stalks. Place, cut-side down, on a baking sheet and cook under the broiler for about 10 minutes, turning them every few minutes until the skin is fully blistered and black all over. Remove the peppers from the oven and seal in a freezer bag. Once cool enough to handle, peel off the skin and slice the flesh into strips.

Slice the tomatoes and lay them on a serving platter, along with the sliced peppers. Sprinkle over plenty of salt and black pepper, then the capers and anchovies. Drizzle with the olive oil and sprinkle with the vinegar. Finish by zesting over the lemon half.

tomates Provençales

Delicious warm or at room temperature, my preferred way of eating these is very simple—on a slice of toasted sourdough bread, spread with goat cheese if I have some. Cooking tomates Provençales is straightforward, but as with all tomato dishes, salt is the most important ingredient: it should be added liberally, since it unlocks their flavor.

Serves 4

10 medium tomatoes

3 garlic cloves, crushed

3 big pinches of sea salt flakes

2 pinches of freshly ground black pepper

20 basil leaves

1–2 tablespoons breadcrumbs

3–4 tablespoons olive oil

Preheat the oven to 425°F (220°C) and slice the tomatoes in half widthways. Place the halves, cut-side up, on a baking pan. Distribute the garlic between the tomatoes, tucking it in so it doesn't sit on the surface.

Sprinkle with plenty of salt and black pepper, followed by the basil leaves and breadcrumbs. Finish with a generous drizzle of olive oil, then bake in the oven for 30–35 minutes, until the tomatoes are oozing and beautiful.

sauce tomate

The easy all-purpose chunky tomato sauce I use in gratins, and on pizzas when I run out of coulis.

Serves 4 (makes about 4¼ cups/1 liter)

¼ cup (60 ml) olive oil

1 tablespoon (½ oz/15 g) butter

1 onion, finely chopped

3 lb 5 oz (1.5 kg) tomatoes

2–3 garlic cloves, finely chopped

½ teaspoon dried thyme

½ teaspoon dried red pepper flakes

2 cups (500 ml) tomato passata or purée

salt and freshly ground black pepper

Add half of the olive oil and all of the butter to a heavy-bottomed saucepan set over medium–low heat. Add the onion and soften, stirring frequently, for 15 minutes. Meanwhile, place the tomatoes in a heatproof bowl and cover with boiling water. After a minute or two, drain the water, peel off the tomato skins, roughly chop, and set aside.

After the onions have been cooking for 15 minutes, add the garlic to the pan, along with the thyme and red pepper flakes. Stir for a minute or two to soften but not brown, then add the tomatoes and turn up the heat a touch. Crush the tomatoes in the pan a little and add plenty of salt and black pepper and the remaining olive oil, then cover with a lid. Fast-simmer for 10 minutes to break down the tomatoes into a sauce, then pour in the passata. Uncover and continue to simmer for 25 minutes, or until you are happy with the consistency.

coulis de tomate à la Provençale

An electric press makes light work of making your own coulis: no peeling and minimal chopping. The result in an "almost ready-made" sauce, delicious but relatively simple and thus adaptable for all kinds of uses: pizzas, stews, soups, gratins. Garlic, olive oil, nigella seeds, and fresh basil or oregano are added when using the sauce, not before. The lemon juice or citric acid is not traditional, but recommended for canning in case your tomatoes are lower in acidity.

Makes about 6¼ quarts (6 liters)

22 lb (10 kg) ripe Roma or San Marzano tomatoes, rinsed and quartered

4 large white onions, roughly chopped

1 large handful coarse sea salt

1 large handful dried thyme

freshly ground black pepper

about ¾ cup (180 ml) bottled lemon juice, or 3 teaspoons citric acid

sugar (optional)

Equipment:

1 tomato press

12 pint-size (16 oz/500 ml) preserving jars

1 extra-large lidded pot (for canning)

Place all the ingredients in the big pan and toss with your hands to coat the tomatoes evenly in the salt and herbs. Place the pan over medium heat and bring to a fast simmer, stirring frequently to prevent the tomatoes from catching on the bottom. Cook for an hour, until reduced by about one-third. Turn off the heat. Place a colander over a large mixing bowl and pour the mixture into the colander, drain briefly to get rid of any excess water, then pour the thick tomato sauce back into the pan.

Assemble your tomato press. Use one of the two remaining mixing bowls to catch the coulis and the other to catch the seeds, skins, and onion pieces that are extracted from the sauce as it is milled. Ladle the tomatoes into the funnel and turn the machine on, using a wooden spoon to drive the tomatoes down the funnel if blockages occur. Discard the bowl of seeds, skins, and onions.

Add 1 tablespoon of bottled lemon juice or ¼ teaspoon of citric acid to each pint-size jar, and carefully ladle the coulis into the jars while it is still hot, ensuring there is ½ inch (1.5 cm) of headspace at the top of each jar. Taste and add a pinch of sugar, if necessary. Cover the jars with the lids

Place a canning rack or clean dish towel in the bottom of your extra-large pot and add as many jars as will fit. Fill with enough hot water to cover the jars by at least 1 inch (2.5 cm). Cover with a lid and bring to a boil over medium heat. Once the water is boiling vigorously, set a timer for 1 hour.*

After an hour, turn off the heat and leave the pot to cool slightly. Remove the jars and allow them to cool very slowly. Once cool, check the seals. If any of the jars haven't sealed, refrigerate and use immediately. Stick a label on the sealed jars indicating the year and the contents (an oft overlooked but important step), and store in a cool dark place: use within a year. Refrigerate after opening.

* Review the USDA Complete Guide to Home Canning for techniques.

trio de salades

There is something to be said for keeping the sides simple at a barbecue, when there is already enough to worry about. Here is a classic French salad trio, adding color and texture to plates piled with meat, and quickly assembled if using pre-cooked or canned chickpeas. Unlike lettuce, these salads can be dressed a little in advance of eating.

Served individually, these each make a substantial first course for 4–5 people.

SALADE DE TOMATES

2¼ lb (1 kg) ripe tomatoes

big pinch of sea salt flakes

1½ teaspoons red wine vinegar

5½ oz (150 g) feta

2 oz (60 g) black olives

⅔ cup (½ oz/15 g) basil leaves

3 tablespoons olive oil

freshly ground black pepper

Wash the tomatoes, then slice and arrange in a single layer on a serving platter. Liberally sprinkle with the salt, followed by the vinegar. Crumble over the feta, then sprinkle over the olives and basil leaves. Finish with a generous drizzle of olive oil and lots of freshly ground black pepper.

CAROTTES RAPÉES

½ garlic clove

1 teaspoon red wine vinegar

1 tablespoon lemon juice

pinch of salt, plus extra if needed

big pinch of freshly ground black pepper

1 heaped teaspoon honey

2 teaspoons walnut oil

¼ cup (60 ml) olive oil

1 lb 5 oz (600 g) carrots, trimmed and peeled

2 teaspoons nigella seeds

Crush the garlic into the base of a salad bowl. Cover with the vinegar and lemon juice. Sprinkle over the pinch of salt and plenty of freshly ground black pepper. Add the honey and mix well, then whisk in the walnut and olive oils.

Using a fine cheese grater (or food processor with grating attachment), grate the carrots and place them in the salad bowl. Toss into the dressing and add extra salt to taste. Finish with a sprinkling of nigella seeds.

SALADE DE POIS CHICHES II

2¾ cups (1 lb 3 oz/550 g) dried chickpeas, or 4 x 14 oz/400 g cans of chickpeas, drained

1 large sweet white onion (or 12 scallions), finely chopped

1 cup (1½ oz/40 g) parsley, finely chopped

1 lb 2 oz (500 g) ripe tomatoes (optional)

¼ cup (60 ml) olive oil

4 teaspoons red wine vinegar

salt and freshly ground black pepper

If using dried chickpeas, soak in water overnight then drian and fast-simmer in plenty of fresh unsalted water until tender, about 40 minutes. Drain and cool.

Place the chickpeas in a salad bowl. Mix in the onion and parsley. Slice and add the tomatoes, if using. Drizzle in the olive oil and vinegar, mix well, then add salt and black pepper to taste.

assiète estivale

summer plate

When purchasing melons, pick ones that are sweet-smelling and heavy relative to their size. This dish is really just a mixture of lovely summery things on one plate, the kind of lunch my publishing girlfriends and I used to make for each other when we met up on weekends to gossip about the office.

Serves 4

4 Tomates Provençales
(see page 74)

1 cantaloupe melon

4 slices of cured ham

10½ oz (300 g) lettuce (such as
Batavia, Romaine, or Gem)

½ baguette (about 22 in/
56 cm long)

5½ oz (150 g) fresh soft goat
cheese (or cream cheese)

4–6 fresh black Mission figs
(approx. 9 oz/250 g), sliced

olive oil

For the salad dressing

pinch of salt

2 teaspoons red wine vinegar

big pinch of freshly ground
black pepper

3 tablespoons olive oil

squeeze of lemon juice

A few hours before you wish to eat, make about a half-quantity of the Tomates Provençales and set on the counter to cool.

Thirty minutes before lunch, prepare the melon: cut into quarters and scrape out the seeds. Halve each quarter again lengthways and peel by sliding a knife along the curve, where the orange flesh meets the rind. Top each piece of melon with half a slice of cured ham. Set aside.

Make the salad dressing: dissolve the salt in the vinegar in a salad bowl. Whisk in the black pepper, olive oil, and lemon juice. Taste to check the seasoning. Wash and dry the lettuce leaves, then place on top of the dressing, followed by the cooled Tomates Provençales. Do not toss. Set aside.

Finally, prepare the fig toasts: slice the baguette and lightly toast. Spread with the goat cheese and top with the figs and a few drops of olive oil. When ready to eat, toss the salad and distribute among four plates, along with the fig toasts and prepared melon. Enjoy.

<figure>
- MELON
- PRODUCTEUR
- FRANCE
</figure>

pizza and pissaladière

The word "Provence" comes from the Romans' denomination for this region, *Provincia Romana*. The Romans left their mark here in the form of roads, aqueducts, and amphitheaters, but perhaps also a love for pizza, since one cannot help notice that if there is a bistro in a village, there is generally also a pizzeria.

Like pizza, truly authentic pissaladière is made with bread dough, which is perhaps why the two are often served side by side at parties in Provence, cut into little squares and piled on platters. The following recipe is for two large, simple tomato pizzas and two large pissaladières. They take a while to make, but as these recipes are thrifty, I find myself coming back to them again and again when entertaining on a budget.

Serves 12,
as an appetizer

For 4 pizza /pissaladière bases

3 tablespoons olive oil

1 teaspoon sugar

2 x ¼ oz (7 g) envelopes instant yeast

7¼ cups (2¼ lb/1 kg) white bread flour, plus extra for dusting

2 teaspoons salt

For 2 pissaladières

7 tablespoons (3½ oz/100 g) butter

4½ lb (2 kg) yellow onions, thinly sliced

7 oz (200 g) drained anchovy fillets (about 5 cans)

5½ oz (150 g) black olives

2 tablespoons olive oil

2 teaspoons dried thyme

salt

Begin by making the dough. Mix the olive oil, sugar, and yeast together in a large mixing bowl. Sift in the flour and salt. Pour in and gradually incorporate 2⅓ cups (550 ml) tepid water into the flour mixture. Work the dough in the bowl for a few minutes, then transfer to a clean surface lightly sprinkled with flour. Knead with clean, lightly floured hands for 15 minutes, until a smooth, springy dough has formed. Shape into a ball and sprinkle with more flour. Place the ball back in the large mixing bowl and cover with plastic. Leave to rise in a warm place while you make the pissaladière and *apéro* pizza toppings.

For the pissaladières: melt the butter in a heavy-bottomed saucepan for which you have a lid over medium heat. Stir in the onions, add a sprinkling of salt and a scant ½ cup (100 ml) of water, and then cover with a lid. Cook the onions for at least 1 hour, stirring frequently. During this stage, the onions must not be allowed to catch; lower the heat if necessary and keep a close watch on the pan. Once the onions are soft and translucent, forming almost a paste, remove the lid and turn the heat up to evaporate any liquid and allow the onions to take on some color. Cook for another 30–45 minutes, stirring frequently, until light brown.

While the onions are cooking, prepare the tomato sauce for the *apéro* pizza topping.

Once the tomato sauce and onions are ready and the dough has risen, preheat the oven to 425°F (220°C). The pizzas and pissaladières will be cooked separately, beginning with the pissaladières.

For 2 *apéro* **pizzas**

½ quantity of Sauce Tomate
(see page 74), or 2 cups (500 ml)
ready-made tomato sauce

1 cup (3½ oz/100 g) grated
Emmental (or chunks of
mozzarella)

½ cup (⅓ oz/10 g) basil leaves

2 teaspoons capers

3 tablespoons olive oil

2 big pinches of freshly ground
black pepper

Punch down the dough. Remove half to make the pissaladières first and cover the remaining dough to make the pizzas at a later stage.

Divide the pissaladière dough among as many baking pans as you are using: ideally, two extra-large pans. Sprinkle flour over the pans then use a small rolling pin and glass tumbler to roll the dough out to the very edge of them. When rolling, sprinkle extra flour over the dough as needed.

Spoon the cooked onions onto the bases, stopping ½ inch (1 cm) from the edge to form a crust. Arrange the anchovies and olives on top of each pissaladière in a crisscross pattern. Finish with a light drizzle of olive oil and a sprinkling of dried thyme. Place the pissaladières in the oven and bake for 20–25 minutes, until the crusts are lightly golden. Once cooked, cool the pissaladières on wire racks, then use scissors to cut into slices and pile onto a serving platter. Cover with foil until you are ready to serve.

To make the pizzas, sprinkle additional flour onto the cooled, extra-large baking pans and split the remaining dough between them. As before, roll out using a small, lightly floured rolling pin and glass tumbler to make bases as wide and thin as possible. When rolling, sprinkle over extra flour as needed.

Divide the tomato sauce between the bases, spreading it up to ½ inch (1 cm) from the edge to form the crust. Sprinkle on the cheese, basil, and capers, and finish with a generous drizzle of olive oil and the black pepper. Bake for 10–15 minutes, until the crusts are lightly golden. Set the pizzas on wire racks to cool, then cut into small slices and pile onto a serving platter. Cover with foil until you are ready to serve.

ratatouille

Ratatouille is a versatile dish. It can be served hot, cold, on its own, as a main or a side, stirred into pappardelle, with barbecues and salads, etc… This recipe serves six as a main course, but will of course go further if used as a side or pasta sauce.

Serves 6–8

¾ cup (180 ml) olive oil

2 yellow onions, roughly chopped

2 peppers (1 red, 1 yellow), deseeded and chopped into 2 inch (5 cm) pieces

2¼ lb (1 kg) eggplants

2¼ lb (1 kg) zucchinis

2 x 14 oz (400 g) cans of whole plum tomatoes

2 bay leaves

big pinch of dried thyme

4 garlic cloves, crushed

salt and freshly ground black pepper

Place a large frying pan over medium–high heat and add 3 tablespoons of the olive oil. Place a large Dutch oven nearby but not over the heat. Fry the onions and peppers together for 15 minutes until softened, stirring almost constantly. Don't allow them to brown: turn down the heat if it looks like this is going to happen.

Prepare the eggplants while the onions and peppers are cooking. Remove the stalks, then chop into 2 inch (5 cm) cubes. Set aside. Once the onions and peppers have softened, add these to the waiting pot.

Add 3 more tablespoons of the olive oil to the frying pan, followed by half of the eggplants. Toss and shake in the pan to coat evenly in the oil, and then cook for 15 minutes, stirring almost constantly. Towards the beginning of the frying process the eggplants can look dry, but don't be tempted to add more oil, simply keep stirring and tossing and they will give off their water eventually and turn glistening, soft, and golden brown in places. Add the first batch of cooked eggplants to the waiting pot, and repeat to cook the remaining half in the same way, using another 3 tablespoons of the olive oil.

Trim and chop the zucchinis into 2 inch (5 cm) chunks. Once you have finished cooking the second batch of eggplants and transferred them to the waiting pot, add the remaining 3 tablespoons of olive oil into the frying pan and add all of the zucchinis. Toss and shake the pan to coat evenly, then fry, stirring constantly for 20 minutes, until cooked through.

Once the zucchinis are cooked, add them to the waiting pot, followed by the canned tomatoes, bay leaves, thyme, garlic, and plenty of salt and black pepper. Mix well, breaking up the tomatoes, and then cover the pot. Place over very low heat and simmer for 1 hour.

After simmering, the ratatouille is ready to serve, or if it is to be served cold, set it aside to cool before chilling in the fridge.

soupe au pistou

My great-aunt Edmée always makes the soupe au pistou. A celebration and symphony of summer vegetables, cooked together but not all at once, it is a dish we anticipate for months: green beans, borlotti beans, tomatoes, zucchinis, all harvested when at their optimum sweetness. Many of us will have contributed in some way to the pot. Edmée may have grown the beans, my uncle Serge the tomatoes, and my grandfather Maxime the bouquet-sized bunches of basil needed for the pistou.

We will meet in Edmée's garden near Carpentras, three generations gathered on the terrace under the dappled shade of a creeping vine. It will be early evening, after the scorching heat has subsided and the cicadas have quietened. Her husband, Roland, serves the *apéro*, Pastis for the adults, mint cordial for the children, toasted almonds for all, and we wait, patiently, for the signal to take our seats. The soup is ready. The broth and vegetables are ladled into bowls, a bright dollop of pistou follows, its fresh acidity and saltiness providing an instant lift to the relative sweetness of the soup on its own. Pistou is different to its Italian cousin pesto in that it does not contain pine nuts, simply pounded basil, garlic, tomato, Parmesan, and olive oil.

Serves 6–8

For the soup

2 tablespoons olive oil

1 onion, finely chopped

2 tomatoes

1 lb 10½ oz (750 g) podded fresh (or 3 x 14 oz/400 g cans of borlotti beans, drained)

2 carrots, diced

2 potatoes, diced

2 zucchinis, diced

10½ oz (300 g) green beans, trimmed and chopped into 2 inch (5 cm) pieces

1½ cups (4¼ oz/120 g) macaroni (or other small pasta, or a mixture of large and small)

salt and freshly ground black pepper

For the pistou

big pinch of salt flakes

5 garlic cloves, peeled

6½ cups (5½ oz/150 g) basil leaves

⅔–¾ cup (150–180 ml) olive oil

1 ripe tomato, peeled

2 oz (60 g) Parmesan, finely grated

freshly ground black pepper

squeeze of lemon juice (optional)

To serve

grated Gruyère, Emmenthal, or Parmesan

For the soup, drizzle the olive oil into a large soup pot over medium–low heat. Add the onion and allow to sweat for 15 minutes until translucent but not brown.

While the onion is cooking, place the tomatoes in a bowl and cover with boiling water. After 1 minute, drain away the water, peel the skins off the tomatoes, and finely chop. After the onion has been cooking for about 8 minutes, add the tomatoes to the pot.

Add the fresh borlotti beans to the pot followed by 17 cups (4 liters) of water. Bring to a boil, then simmer the beans for 30 minutes, or until tender, while you prepare the remaining vegetables. (If using canned borlotti beans, there is, of course, no need to simmer them for 30 minutes, simply drain and add with the other vegetables directly).

Once the borlotti beans are tender, add the carrots and potatoes to the pot and simmer together for 15–20 minutes. Add the zucchinis and green beans and simmer for a further 10–15 minutes. Taste and season with salt and black pepper. (At this point, the soup can be turned off and set aside for a few hours, then slowly reheated before cooking the macaroni in it.)

Once the vegetables are all simmering together in the pot, prepare the pistou: place the big pinch of salt flakes in a large mortar with the garlic cloves and pound to a paste. Add the basil leaves, and then gradually add ⅔ cup (150 ml) of the olive oil, followed by the tomato, pounding as you go, until you have a lovely pistou. Stir in the grated Parmesan last, then taste to check the seasoning. Add black pepper, more olive oil, or a squeeze of lemon juice, if necessary.

To finish and serve the soup, 30 minutes before you are ready to eat, add the macaroni. The pasta will take longer to cook than usual since the soup should only be gently simmering. Once the macaroni is ready, bring the pot to the table. Ladle the soup into bowls, then top each with a generous tablespoon of pistou and some grated cheese. Toast the summer.

Tata Edmée's eggplant gratin

Tata Edmée's eggplant gratin is one of the rare recipes we consider worth the discomfort of turning on the oven in the height of summer. This absolutely delicious vegetarian main course uses relatively few ingredients, so is worth making with organic eggplants if this is within the household budget.

   If I am really going to town on a meal for friends, I would serve this with a roasted leg of lamb. The eggplants and tomato sauce can be pre-cooked the day before and the gratin assembled just before going into the oven. The final bake brings out the overall sweetness of the dish.

Serves 6

4½ lb (2 kg) eggplants

3–4 teaspoons salt

1 quantity of Sauce Tomate (see page 74), or 4¼ cups (1 liter) ready-made tomato sauce

4¼ cups (1 liter) peanut oil

¾ cup (3 oz/80 g) grated Parmesan

Begin by preparing the eggplants a few hours before you wish to make your gratin. Slice off the stalks and peel the eggplants entirely. Cut lengthways into whole pieces ¾ inch (2 cm) thick. Place the slices in a colander over a mixing bowl and sprinkle with a good few teaspoons of salt, tossing with your hands to coat evenly. Set aside for a few hours to draw the moisture out of the eggplants. Any discoloration is of no consequence since they are going to be deep-fried later.

While the eggplants are salting, prepare the tomato sauce as per the instructions on page 74.

After a few hours, once the eggplants have given off quite a few tablespoons of liquid, fill a wide, heavy sauté pan with ¾–1¼ inches (2–3 cm) of peanut oil. Place over medium–high heat and position a plate nearby, covered with a few layers of paper towels. After 5–10 minutes, once the oil is hot, pick up an eggplant slice, brush off any excess salt, give it a final squeeze over the sink to remove any further moisture and, using tongs, carefully lower into the hot oil. Repeat until you have filled but not overcrowded the pan: there should only be one layer of eggplants cooking at a time. Turn your eggplant slices after a minute or two, then, once golden brown all over, remove from the pan, one by one, using tongs or a slotted spoon, and place on the plate of paper towels. Repeat these steps until you have cooked all the eggplant slices.

The gratin can now be assembled: preheat the oven to 400°F (200°C). Spoon a layer of tomato sauce over the base of a lasagne dish or large pie dish, then cover with a layer of eggplants, followed by a generous sprinkle of Parmesan. Repeat until you have used up all the eggplants, finishing with a layer of tomato sauce and a generous final sprinkling of Parmesan.

Bake for 45 minutes, then serve.

Tata Régine's fried eggplants

My great-aunt Tata Régine wrote down some of her recipes before she passed away. We smile now at some of her recipes, written in beautiful handwriting in pencil: *"Prendre un bon kilo d'eggplants."* What is a "good" kilo? Did she mean more than a kilo? Or more lyrically, *"Cueillir une belle tomate."* … Thankfully, the memory of a dish and knowing how something tasted goes a fair way towards trying to recreate it. Tata Régine would spend afternoons deep-frying vast quantities of eggplants from her garden to make this, a classic "Régine" appetizer at one of the many family banquets she hosted. The eggplants can be served at room temperature or chilled, and thus made ahead.

Serves 6,
as an appetizer

2¼ lb (1 kg) eggplants

1 tablespoon salt

4¼ cups (1 liter) peanut oil

¼ cup (⅓ oz/10 g) finely chopped parsley

baguette, to serve

Wash the eggplants, slice off the stalks, and peel entirely. Cut lengthways into ¾ inch (2 cm) thick slices. Place in a colander over a mixing bowl and sprinkle over a good amount of salt, tossing with your hands to coat evenly. Set aside for 1–2 hours to draw out as much moisture as possible.

Once the eggplants have given off quite a few tablespoons of liquid, fill a wide sauté pan with ¾–1¼ inches (2–3 cm) of peanut oil. Place over medium–high heat and position a plate nearby, covered with a few layers of paper towels.

After 5–10 minutes, once the oil is hot enough, pick up an eggplant slice, brush off any excess salt, and give it a firm squeeze over the sink to remove any further water. Using tongs, carefully lower into the hot oil. Repeat the squeezing steps until you have filled but not overcrowded the pan: there should only be one layer of eggplant cooking at a time. Turn the slices after a few minutes and, once golden brown all over, remove from the pan, one by one, using tongs, and place on the waiting plate of paper towels. Repeat the steps until you have cooked all of the eggplant slices.

Lay the slices on a serving platter and sprinkle with the finely chopped parsley. Serve as they are, with fresh baguette.

gratin de pommes de terres aux tomates

tomato and potato gratin

"La Cousine de notre grand-mère Rose, dite Tante Adèle était partie travailler sur la Côte d'Azur où il y avait déjà des milliardaires Russes et Anglais. Elle est devenue cuisinière et son mari palefrenier. C'est d'elle que nous avons récolté la fameuse recette du Gratin de Pommes de Terres aux Tomates qui est d'ailleurs une recette de la région de Nice. Voici la Recette:" **Régine Trescarte**

We found this note written by Tata Régine above her recipe for this delicious tomato and potato gratin, dutifully crediting its origins from the cooks and kitchens of the grand houses on the Côte d'Azur in the 1930s.

Serves 4–6

3 onions, chopped

about ½ cup (120 ml) olive oil

1 lb 2 oz (500 g) potatoes, peeled and sliced into ⅛ inch (3 mm) thick rounds

2 teaspoons dried thyme

2 bay leaves

½ cup (¾ oz/20 g) finely chopped parsley

8 tomatoes

3 garlic cloves, crushed

1⅔ cups (400 ml) chicken or vegetable stock

salt and freshly ground black pepper

Preheat the oven to 425°F (220°C). Find a beautiful, large earthenware gratin dish. Spread the chopped onion in the base of the dish. Cover with 2 tablespoons of the olive oil and mix.

Layer half of the sliced potatoes on top of the onions. Sprinkle on plenty of salt and black pepper, half of the thyme, and one bay leaf, then add another tablespoon of the olive oil. Place the remaining potatoes on top of the first layer, and again, sprinkle over salt, black pepper, and the remaining thyme and bay leaf, and add three-quarters of the chopped parsley.

Wash the tomatoes and slice off their tops. Cut and scoop out any core that looks firm, then place the tomatoes on top of the potatoes, open-side up. Sprinkle over plenty of salt and black pepper. Distribute the garlic between the hollows, followed by the remaining parsley. Finish by drizzling at least ½ tablespoon of olive oil inside each tomato.

Pour the stock into the base of the dish over the potatoes. Place the dish in the oven and bake for 1 hour. Oven temperatures vary so if the tops of the potatoes brown very quickly, lower the temperature to 400°F (200°C) for the final 30 minutes. Serve immediately.

tomates farcies

For this Provençal classic, a deep, large oven or lasagne dish is necessary: ideally about 2 inches (5 cm) high, large enough to accommodate all the tomatoes comfortably, leaving a little space in between for the rice. My grandfather tells me that they were eating tomates farcies when the Germans started bombing the fields in front of the farm—the Nazis were doing random target practice, firing from miles away, near Sault. I suppose that sort of event would make a meal memorable.

Serves 4,
as a main course

½ oz (15 g) white baguette or country bread (fresh or stale)

scant ½ cup (100 ml) milk

5 tablespoons olive oil, plus extra for drizzling

1 onion, finely chopped

1 teaspoon fennel seeds

8 extra-large tomatoes, 7–9 oz (200–250 g) each

1 lb 5 oz (600 g) sausage meat (or good-quality sausages)

2 tablespoons finely chopped parsley leaves

1 egg

½ cup (3 oz/80 g) long-grain white rice

salt and freshly ground black pepper

Preheat the oven to 425°F (220°C). Place the bread in a bowl and submerge in the milk.

Heat 3 tablespoons of the olive oil in a frying pan over low–medium heat and add the chopped onion. Bash the fennel seeds using a mortar and pestle and add to the pan. Cook, stirring frequently, for about 15 minutes until the onion is soft.

Meanwhile, slice the tops off the tomatoes and set aside. Scoop out the inner tomato flesh to make room for the stuffing. Discard any hard cores and finely chop the flesh. Add this to the pan of onion after it has been frying for at least 10 minutes, sprinkle on some salt and black pepper, and add another tablespoon of the olive oil. Cook together for 5 minutes, then leave to cool.

Place the sausage meat in a large bowl (squeezing out the meat from the sausages, if using). Squeeze the bread dry (discarding the milk) and finely chop. Add to the bowl of meat, together with the parsley. Crack in the egg, then add the cooked onion and tomato flesh. Mix with your hands.

Drizzle the base of a deep large oven dish with 1 tablespoon of the olive oil and arrange the hollowed tomatoes inside. Spoon the meat mixture into the cavities, then put the tops back on the tomatoes. Add a final drizzle of olive oil over the top, then place in the oven.

After 30 minutes, take the dish out of the oven. Sprinkle the rice in the spaces between the tomatoes, where lots of succulent juices will have gathered. Cook for another 15–20 minutes, until the rice is fully cooked. Serve immediately with a delicious green salad.

wild rice and eggplants

This is a very delicious main course on its own, but if I am cooking something of a feast, I would serve it with the Spatchcocked Poussins (see page 103).

Serves 4–6

For the rice

1 cup (7 oz/200 g) French green lentils

1 cup (7 oz/200 g) mixed wild, basmati, and Camargue rice

1 lb 5 oz (600 g) eggplants, chopped into 2 inch (5 cm) chunks

¼ cup (60 ml) olive oil

3 tablespoons (1½ oz/40 g) butter

2 onions, thinly sliced

2 cinnamon sticks

4¼ cups (1 liter) chicken stock

sea salt flakes and freshly ground black pepper

For the yogurt sauce

½ garlic clove, peeled

1 cup (9 oz/250 g) plain or Greek yogurt

½ lemon

2 tablespoons finely chopped fresh mint or parsley leaves

salt and freshly ground black pepper

Soak the lentils and rice together for 1 hour in tepid water.

Preheat the oven to 425°F (220°C). Place the eggplant chunks on a baking pan. Brush with olive oil, sprinkle with salt and black pepper, and bake for 35–40 minutes, tossing them a few times to prevent them from sticking, until dark golden brown. Remove from the oven and set aside.

Meanwhile, melt the butter over medium heat in an extra-large sauté pan for which you have a lid. Add the onions and cinnamon and cook for 15 minutes, until soft and starting to turn golden brown and lightly crisp in places. Stir in the drained lentils and rice, followed by the stock, then cover the pan and simmer for 25 minutes. Remove the lid and check the rice and lentils are cooked. If they are ready, remove the lid and allow any excess liquid to evaporate.

Prepare the yogurt sauce: crush the garlic into a bowl and add the yogurt, a squeeze of lemon juice, and some salt and black pepper. Taste to check the seasoning, then stir in the mint or parsley.

Once all the elements are ready, spoon the cooked rice and lentils onto a serving platter. Arrange the roasted eggplants on top, and spoon the yogurt sauce all over. Enjoy warm or at room temperature.

green beans

In Provence, green beans are eaten very tender, almost melt-in-the-mouth. In fact, my grandfather will complain that they are "undercooked" if there is any bite in them at all. Try them like this, boiled then cooked with butter and garlic, alongside a rare steak or grilled fish, and you won't look back.

Serves 4–6

2¼ lb (1 kg) green beans, trimmed

3½ tablespoons (1¾ oz/50 g) butter

2 garlic cloves, minced

salt and freshly ground black pepper

Bring a large pan of salted water to a boil. Add the green beans and boil for at least 10 minutes, until completely tender and floppy. Drain in a colander and set aside.

Melt the butter in a large sauté pan over medium heat. Add the green beans and garlic. Toss together gently and cook for a further 5 minutes, stirring continuously, until the beans are lovely, glistening, and melt-in-the-mouth. Sprinkle with salt and black pepper to taste before bringing the dish to the table.

zucchini rigatoni

My uncle Serge grows countless vegetables in the fields behind his house. He can never give away enough and comes by the house a few times a week, shouting "*Vé, vé vé!*" in Provençal with cases of freshly picked zucchinis and zucchini flowers. This pasta dish is one of our favorites. Zucchini flowers can be tricky (and expensive) to find if the zucchinis aren't home grown, so omit them from this recipe if this is the case.

Serves 3–4

2 tablespoons sunflower oil

2 lb 10 oz (1.2 kg) zucchinis (8–10 medium), sliced into ⅛ inch (3 mm) thick rounds

1½ teaspoons freshly ground black pepper, plus more if needed

1 teaspoon red pepper flakes

2 handfuls zucchini flowers (optional)

zest and juice of 1 lemon

10½ oz (300 g) rigatoni (about 4 cups)

1¼ cups (4¼ oz/120 g) grated Grana Padano, plus more if needed

3 tablespoons olive oil

⅔ cup (½ oz/15 g) basil leaves, sliced

salt

Place the sunflower oil a large frying or sauté pan over medium heat. Add the zucchinis and sprinkle with plenty of salt and the pepper and red pepper flakes.

Toss the zucchinis in the pan to coat evenly in the oil, then cover the pan and soften for 20 minutes, stirring every few minutes. Remove the lid and sauté for a further 15 minutes, standing by and tossing frequently, until the zucchinis have become very soft and taken on some color. During this time, bring a large saucepan of salted water to a boil.

Once the zucchinis are almost done, stir in the flowers and lemon zest. Sauté for 1 minute. Add the pasta to the pan of boiling water. Sauté the zucchinis together with the zucchini flowers and lemon zest for a final few minutes, stirring almost constantly, then turn the heat down to a minimum while the pasta cooks (according to the package instructions).

Drain and transfer the cooked pasta, with a little of its cooking water, to the pan of zucchinis and immediately pour in the lemon juice, grated cheese, olive oil, and basil leaves. Toss for a few minutes in the pan to coat evenly, and crucially, taste to check the seasoning, adding more salt, black pepper, lemon juice, or cheese if necessary. Serve immediately.

panisses and shrimp

When I moved back to Provence, I decided that the best way to arrive would be by bicycle. I bicycled all the way down from England and for some reason the journey was book-ended by meals of cooked shrimp: the first was eaten on the ferry from Portsmouth to the Finistère, accompanied by mayonnaise, sliced baguette, and a bottle of Breton cider for courage. Three weeks, twenty-one campsites, and 930 miles (1500 km) later, I sat on a shaded restaurant terrace in Marseille with fellow cyclist Felicity Cloake, wondering how on earth we had managed it, eating shrimp once again, this time with panisses, tomato salad, and a very large pitcher of Provençal rosé: I had arrived *au Sud*.

Panisses are traditional Provençal chickpea flour "fries," cut from a prepared, chilled batter and deep-fried. Prepare the batter a day or two in advance and keep it in the fridge until ready to cook. Here I serve them with delicious cooked shrimp and a salad.

Since you need to set up a deep-frying station here anyway, it may be worth also making the Accras de Morue (see page 101). Conversely, if you don't want to deep-fry the panisses, they could be drizzled with olive oil, sprinkled with salt, and oven-baked, though the texture and flavor will not be the same.

Serves 6

For the panisses

4¼ cups (1 liter) water

3 tablespoons olive oil

1 heaped teaspoon salt

1 garlic clove, crushed

3 cups (10½ oz/300 g) chickpea flour

pinch of cayenne pepper

6⅓ cups (1.5 liters) sunflower oil

To serve

generous ¾ cup (200 ml) Aïoli Mayonnaise (see page 198)

1 medium-large ripe tomato, sliced

½ head Romaine lettuce, leaves separated

2¼ lb (1 kg) shell-on cooked shrimp

Cont'd overleaf.

Make the panisses batter: line a large rectangular gratin or pie dish with plastic. Place the water in a large, stainless steel saucepan. Add the olive oil, salt, and garlic, then stir and bring to a boil. Once bubbling, turn the heat off and immediately add the chickpea flour and cayenne pepper. Use a handheld immersion blender to mix for 5 minutes until you have obtained a completely smooth, thick batter.

Place the batter back over low heat and beat with a wooden spoon for 10 minutes: this is a tedious but necessary part of the process to release the starch and stop your panisses falling apart during frying.

After you have beaten the batter for 10 minutes, spoon into the plastic-lined dish, and smooth the surface. Cool on the counter before chilling in the fridge for at least 3 hours, until completely set. The batter can happily sit in the fridge for 2 days after this point.

Towards the end of the chilling time, prepare the aïoli mayonnaise as on page 198. Make the salad by whisking the dressing ingredients (overleaf) in a large salad bowl and topping with the tomato slices and lettuce leaves. Do not toss until you are ready to serve. Place the shrimp on a serving platter and keep in the fridge until you are about to eat.

For the salad dressing

3 tablespoons olive oil

1 tablespoon red wine vinegar

salt and freshly ground black pepper

Pour the sunflower oil into an extra-large heavy-bottomed saucepan (for safety, ensure the oil only comes one-third to halfway up the pan) and place over medium heat. Wait at least 10 minutes for the oil to heat before beginning to deep-fry your panisses.

While the oil is heating, line another serving plate with paper towels for the deep-fried panisses. Remove the batter from the fridge and use a knife and spatula to remove sections and cut into chunky "fry" shapes.

Once the oil is hot enough (test it by putting a small piece of batter in: it should bubble fairly fiercely), use a spatula or slotted spoon to carefully lower a few panisses at a time into the oil. Aim to fill but not overcrowd the pan. Deep-fry for 1 minute, until lightly golden all over (you may need to turn the panisses if the level of oil in your pan requires it). Then lift them out of the oil using a slotted spoon or spatula and transfer to the lined plate. Cover with foil, then begin deep-frying the next batch. Continue until you have used up all the batter, keeping the cooked panisses warm under plenty of foil. Serve with the aïoli mayonnaise, the tossed salad, the platter of shrimp, and a plate for the empty shrimp shells. Once completely cooled, the frying oil can be rebottled, and reused, if desired.

accras de morue

I traveled to Martinique in 1989 with my parents to visit my uncle, aunt, and cousins. Tonton Bernard was in the French Navy and it was while he was stationed there that my aunt Tati Véro learned this French Caribbean recipe for salt cod fritters. She continued to make them when they returned to Provence. The portable gas stove was set up outside on the terrace to avoid heating up the house and she would deep-fry them to have as an informal apéritif. We would eat them with our fingers almost as soon as they touched the paper towels.

Serves 6,
as an appetizer

14 oz (400 g) salt cod fillet, soaked for 24 hours in frequent changes of water (or use smoked haddock fillet)

2 bay leaves

2 cups (9 oz/250 g) all-purpose flour

1 teaspoon baking powder

2 teaspoons cayenne pepper

2 teaspoons ground cumin

2 teaspoons freshly ground black pepper

3 eggs

⅔ cup (150 ml) milk

2 shallots, finely chopped

⅔ cup (1 oz/30 g) chopped parsley

2 garlic cloves, crushed

6⅓–8½ cups (1.5–2 liters) peanut oil

fresh lemon juice or Aïoli Mayonnaise (see page 198), to serve

Boil a large saucepan of water. Drain the cod and add to the boiling water, together with the bay leaves. Lower the heat and simmer for 10 minutes. Once the flesh is opaque and flakes apart with ease, drain and place in a colander to cool while you prepare the accras batter.

Place the flour, baking powder, and spices in a mixing bowl and make a well in the center. Crack in the eggs and add the milk, shallots, parsley, and garlic. Mix well, cover, and set aside for 30 minutes at room temperature (or overnight in the fridge if preparing the batter in advance).

While the batter is resting, check the cooled fish for any bones, then mash to a paste. This can be done on a chopping board with the back of a fork or using a large mortar and pestle.

When you are ready to serve, place the peanut oil in a deep large saucepan over medium–high heat. You need about 3 inches (7.5 cm) of oil in the pan, but do ensure the pan is appropriately sized since the oil level should not come more than a third of the way up for safety reasons. It will take at least 5 minutes for the oil to become hot enough to deep-fry the accras.

While the oil is heating, line a serving plate with paper towels. Stir the mashed fish into the batter and mix well. Once the oil is hot enough, gently drop a modest tablespoon of accras batter into the pan (you will likely need a second spoon to coax the batter off the first). Continue adding tablespoons of batter, until you are cooking about five accras. Never leaving the pan unattended, deep-fry the accras for about 3 minutes. Once golden brown all over, transfer to the lined plate using a slotted spoon or spatula and begin spooning in the next batch. Repeat the previous steps until you have deep-fried all the batter.

Serve immediately with fresh lemon juice or aïoli mayonnaise.

les grillades

A barbecue in Provence, known as *les grillades*, generally means two things: lamb chops and merguez. *Les grillades* are almost always wood-fired and piles of old vines are kept outside farms and houses for this purpose: their flames are short-lived and turn quickly to embers, perfect for barbecues though not for heating homes. On the old farm, *les grillades* were cooked indoors over an open fireplace in a room we called *la cuisine de Jules*. The ceiling beams housed many swallows' nests and the walls were blackened with soot. The eponymous Jules was a much-loved farmhand, who lived and worked with my family all his life. He loved his *grillades*.

You can occasionally source merguez, delicious North African spiced lamb and beef sausages, from butchers, but they are not an everyday supermarket find. The recipe below for Merguez Koftas hits similar notes, though I would encourage you to seek out the real deal if only to try once.

Serves 4

1 egg

splash of milk

2 tablespoons olive oil

2 garlic cloves, finely chopped

1 teaspoon dried garlic

1 heaped tablespoon tomato paste

1 tablespoon store-bought harissa paste

2 teaspoons cayenne pepper

1 teaspoon ground coriander

1½ teaspoons ground cumin

1 teaspoon smoked paprika

pinch of freshly grated nutmeg

1 lb 2 oz (500 g) ground lamb or beef

vegetable oil (if cooking indoors)

salt and freshly ground black pepper

MERGUEZ KOFTAS

Delicious with Mint, Yogurt, and Cucumber Dip (see page 199). These could also be shaped into burgers and served with bread.

Whisk the egg, milk, and olive oil together in a large mixing bowl. Add the garlic to the bowl, along with the tomato paste, harissa, all the spices, and salt and black pepper to your liking. Whisk, then once fully mixed, crumble in the meat, then combine the mixture with your hands. Cover and place the bowl in the fridge until you are ready to cook.

Form a large golf-ball-sized amount of the mixture into a sausage-like kofta shape. Continue forming koftas while you preheat the barbecue or frying pan.

To barbecue: once the barbecue is hot, place as many koftas as will fit directly on the grill and cook for 6–8 minutes in total, turning so they cook evenly.

To cook indoors: add 2 tablespoons of sunflower oil to a frying pan over medium–high heat. Once hot, add as many koftas as will fit in the pan without packing it too tightly. Cook for about 8 minutes, turning once halfway through. Place the cooked koftas on a serving platter and cover with foil while you cook the next batch.

Serves 6

(½ poussin per person)

3 poussins

2 tablespoons coarse sea salt flakes

vegetable oil (if cooking indoors)

For the marinade

1 lemon

4 cloves

1 teaspoon freshly ground black pepper

1 tablespoon dried thyme

2 tablespoons olive oil

3 garlic cloves, crushed

1 cup (9 oz/250 g) plain yogurt

SPATCHCOCKED POUSSINS

Serve with Wild Rice and Eggplants (see page 94) for a very special meal.

Half a day before you wish to serve, spatchcock the poussins. Lay a bird on a chopping board, breast-side down, with the legs closest to you. Using scissors, cut along either side of the backbone. Discard the backbone and push the sides of the bird down so it sits as flat as possible (making an incision in the neck can also help). Flip the bird over, then push the body in a downwards motion to flatten even further. Rub sea salt flakes all over, then place in a bowl and repeat with the other two poussins.

Once all three birds are spatchcocked, prepare the marinade: Squeeze the juice from the lemon into a mixing bowl. Grind the cloves using a mortar and pestle and add to the mixing bowl, along with the black pepper, thyme, olive oil, garlic, and yogurt. Mix well, then place the birds in the bowl and rub all over with the marinade. Cover and refrigerate for 4 hours.

To barbecue: Light the barbecue and, once it's hot, place the poussins directly on the grill. Cook for 10 minutes on each side. Check the juices run clear before serving.

To cook indoors: Preheat the oven to 350°F (180°C). Place two frying pans over medium heat, add 1 tablespoon of sunflower oil to each, and brown the birds for 5 minutes on each side. Place on a baking pan and roast for 20–25 minutes. Ensure the juices run clear before serving.

sardines

Sardines are both delicious and economical, and take mere moments to cook.

Serves 4

1¾ lb (800 g) fresh, whole, gutted sardines

1 lemon

2 tablespoons olive oil (if cooking indoors)

To barbecue: Light the barbecue and, once it's hot, place the sardines in a fish grill basket, so they can be easily turned. Cook for 2 minutes on one side, then 1 minute on the other. Place the sardines on a serving platter, grate over some lemon zest, and squeeze over a little lemon juice. Serve immediately

To cook indoors: Turn the broiler on high. Lay the sardines on a raised grill rack on a baking pan. Grate over some lemon zest and drizzle with the olive oil. Place under the broiler for 2–3 minutes. Turn once, then cook for a final 1 minute. Place the sardines on a serving platter, squeeze on some lemon juice, and serve immediately.

ventoux sandwich

There is a tradition in these parts to climb to the 6273 foot (1912 m) summit of the Mont Ventoux in a night to watch the sunrise. Such walks usually take place in June, when the nights are shortest, starting from the town of Bedoin at about midnight. My grandfather tells me that when he and his sisters would do it in the late 1940s and early 1950s, they would pack an egg sandwich to eat at the top, while they waited for a ride back down.

Serves 2

3 eggs

4¾ oz (135 g) can of sardines

2 small tomatoes

1 fresh baguette (about 22 in/ 56 cm long)

butter

1 teaspoon freshly ground black pepper

8 cornichons

salt

Place the eggs in a pan of boiling water and cook for 9 minutes. Allow the eggs to cool, then peel and slice. Drain the sardines, halve lengthways, and remove the bony spines. Slice the tomatoes and sprinkle a little salt over them.

Slice open the baguette lengthways, remove any excess soft dough, and spread liberally with butter. Add plenty of black pepper, then fill the sandwich with the sardines, eggs, tomatoes, and cornichons. Halve the sandwich and wrap in foil for later, or eat immediately.

fig and rose ice cream

Rosewater conjures images of the Middle East and its beautiful desserts, but Provence is also a well-known cultivator of this flower for its perfumed oil near the town of Grasse. Rosewater is a by-product of the oil distillation process.

Serves 6–8

1 cup (250 ml) whole milk

¾ cup (5½ oz/150 g) sugar

5 egg yolks

1 cup (250 ml) heavy whipping cream

12 oz (350 g) fresh figs, very finely chopped

2 teaspoons rosewater

Add the milk and half of the sugar to a pan set over medium heat. Stir until the sugar has dissolved and continue to heat until little bubbles appear on the side of the pan. Turn the heat off.

Place the egg yolks in a bowl and add the remaining sugar. Whisk until the mixture turns pale. Pour this into the pan of warmed milk, place over the lowest heat, and cook for 10 minutes, stirring often and making sure it doesn't ever bubble fiercely. It should form a custard thick enough to coat the back of your spoon. Remove from the heat, cover with plastic wrap to prevent a skin from forming, and allow to cool.

Gently whip the cream in a large bowl that will also fit in your freezer. Don't over-whip, simply aim to thicken the cream a little. Pour the cooled custard into the bowl of whipped cream and stir in the figs and rosewater. Place the mixing bowl in the freezer and stir every 30 minutes for 3–4 hours, after which the ice cream will be ready to scoop and serve, or decant into a lidded container, seal tightly, and return to the freezer. Enjoy within a month.

pêches au vin

baked peaches in wine

When stone fruit is past its best, it can be improved with stewing or baking. In this recipe, the peaches can be substituted for fresh apricots, plums, or cherries, the cinnamon for orange or lemon zest, the wine for cognac or Grand Marnier… This dish should be placed in the oven to cook about 15 minutes before sitting down to eat so it can be served hot for dessert: three peach halves per person, served on their own, with ice cream, or with crème fraîche and slivered almonds.

Serves 4

6 peaches, halved and pitted

1½ tablespoons sugar

pinch of ground cinnamon

3 tablespoons red wine

Preheat the oven to 400°F (200°C). Place the peaches on a baking pan, cut-side up, and sprinkle with the sugar and cinnamon. Pour the red wine into the hollows and over the peaches. Bake in the oven for 30 minutes. Serve immediately with ice cream or crème fraîche

yogurt and apricot ice cream

Yogurt ice cream is best eaten within a week since it does not keep as well as traditional ice cream. It is, however, a lot easier to make.

Serves 6–8

heaped 1 cup (5½ oz/150 g) dried apricots, or 7 oz (200 g) fresh apricots, pitted

½ cup (125 ml) heavy whipping cream

generous 2 cups (1 lb 2 oz/ 500 g) plain whole milk yogurt

½ cup (3½ oz/100 g) sugar

Chop the apricots as finely as you can (or blend in a blender with a few spoonfuls of the yogurt if a smoother finish is preferable).

Gently whip the cream in a large mixing bowl. Fold in the yogurt, sugar, and chopped apricots. Place the bowl in the freezer and stir every 30 minutes for 2½–3 hours. The yogurt ice cream will then be ready to scoop and serve.

confiture d'abricots

apricot jam

During school vacations on the big farm, my cousins and I would leap out of bed to the sound of the cockerel harassing the poor hens outside and dash downstairs to make ourselves some breakfast. Then, accompanied by Marquis the dog, we would begin a morning of adventures. Bicycle races through the vines, hide-and-seek in the forests, terrifying each other with pretend sightings of wild boars, and building countless *cabanes* (forts). A good *petit déjeuner* was important: invariably hot chocolate and a slice of baguette slathered in butter and apricot jam.

The simplest recipes are often the best, and most of the time I make this jam with apricots, sugar, and nothing else. Adding an aromatic like rosemary or lemon zest is lovely every so often, however, when I really want to have fun with this, I'll simmer the jam over a barbecue to give it a smoky flavor.

Makes approx. 5 cups (1.2 liters)

3 lb 5 oz (1.5 kg) apricots, halved and pitted

1 large lemon

sprig of rosemary or lavender (optional)

4½ cups (2 lb/900 g) sugar

Equipment:

5 sterilized half-pint (8 oz/ 250 ml) preserving jars

1 extra-large lidded pot (for canning)

Place the apricots in a large lidded pan. Peel and add the lemon rind, followed by all of the lemon juice. Add the sprig of rosemary or lavender, if using.

Cover the pan and warm over low heat. Gently stew the fruit for 1½ hours, stirring frequently, until lovely and liquidy.

Add the sugar, stir to dissolve, then simmer, uncovered, keeping a close eye on the pan and stirring frequently, until the jam thickens and turns a lovely amber color. Funnel the jam into the jars while it is still hot, ensuring there is ½ inch (1.5 cm) of headspace at the top of each jar. Cover with the lids.

Place a clean dish towel or canning rack at the bottom of your extra-large pot and add as many jars as will fit. Fill with enough hot water to cover the jars by at least 1 inch (2.5 cm). Cover with a lid and bring to a boil over medium heat. Once the water is boiling vigorously, set a timer for 10 minutes.*

After this time, turn off the heat and leave the pot to cool slightly. Remove the jars and allow them to cool very slowly. Once cool, check the seals. If any of the jars haven't sealed, refrigerate and use immediately. Stick a label on the sealed jars and store in a cool dark place: use within a year. Refrigerate after opening.

* Review the USDA Complete Guide to Home Canning for techniques.

plum chutney

Making chutney is an opportunity to use up any spices or unloved fruit vinegars that have been languishing in your pantry for some time. There is no need to be too precious about the type of vinegar used and you can combine a few, for example apple cider and white wine vinegars, to make up the quantity required. The French don't have a cheese and chutney tradition, unfortunately, but the plum chutney I make every year has infiltrated the hallowed ranks of our Provence Christmas Day menu: we serve it with foie gras or chicken liver pâté.

The plum tree outside the cottage my great-grandmother lived in on the big farm is overshadowed by illustrious neighbors: fig and jujube trees worthy of paradise gardens. Nevertheless, one year, I borrowed an orchard ladder from the hangar and picked the bucketful of plums that was to become the best chutney I have ever made.

Makes approx. 6⅓ cups (1.5 liters)

4½ lb (2 kg) plums, pitted and roughly chopped

2 large onions, finely chopped

2¾ cups (650 ml) vinegar

1 tablespoon ground allspice

1 tablespoon ground cumin

1 tablespoon ground coriander

2 teaspoons mustard seeds

1 teaspoon ground cinnamon

1 teaspoon ground cloves

½ teaspoon ground nutmeg

1½ cups (10½ oz/300 g) sugar

Equipment:

6 (or more—it can't hurt) sterilized half-pint (8 oz/250 ml) preserving jars

1 extra-large lidded pot (for canning)

Place the plums in a large saucepan. Then add the onions, along with the vinegar and spices.

Place over medium heat and cover. Bring to a fast simmer, then uncover and lower the heat. Gently simmer for about 1 hour, stirring frequently using a wooden spoon and crushing the plums a little as you do.

Once the fruit is stewed, add the sugar and stir until dissolved. Simmer, uncovered, for a further 20 minutes, stirring frequently, until the chutney has a thick consistency. Ladle the chutney into the jars while it is still hot, ensuring there is ½ inch (1.5 cm) of headspace at the top of each jar. Cover with the lids.

Place a clean dish towel or canning rack at the bottom of your extra-large pot and add as many jars as will fit. Fill with enough hot water to cover the jars by at least 1 inch (2.5 cm). Cover with a lid and bring to a boil over medium heat. Once the water is boiling, set a timer for 10 minutes.*

After this time, turn off the heat and leave the pot to cool slightly. Remove the jars and allow them to cool very slowly. Once cool, check the seals. If any of the jars haven't sealed, refrigerate and use immediately. Stick a label on the sealed jars and store in a cool dark place: use within a year. Refrigerate after opening.

* Review the USDA Complete Guide to Home Canning for techniques.

"Une journée sans vin est une journée sans soleil."
Provençal proverb

autumn

AUTUMN AWAKENS AN INDUSTRIOUSNESS HITHERTO DORMANT IN ME, more so than
at New Years, no doubt a relic of new school years past. It is a time for invigorated
routines. I find myself sitting at the kitchen table, making a list of what is to be done
over the coming weeks. Tomato coulis, jams, and chutneys first. Later, quince cheese,
sloe gin, vin d'orange, and olives. The list is considerable but so are the rewards.

There is other work, too. In London, a nine to five. In Provence, the grape harvest,
or vendanges, in the fields from eight am until four pm. Thoughtfully prepared
packed lunches and quick and satisfying evening meals are in order. There are
the hot soups to greet us at home as the temperatures cool. The stews and daubes,
prepared a day in advance for gentle reheating when needed. The aromatic slow
roasts of weekends as we draw inside our homes.

But in between all of this, there is the list. In Provence, it is a necessary drive to
preserve as much of our produce as possible. When I am far from home, it is part of a
deep desire within me to remain connected to my family's harvests, and I know many
of my fellow urbanites and friends love to mark the season this way too. We buy our
ingredients in bulk from unpretentious markets. We set about preparing lovely things
and our pantries are soon joyfully replete with preserves and liqueurs for the coming
winter months. The majority of us won't have vast quantities of home-grown produce
to save, and no one is forcing any of us to make any of these products ourselves. Yet if
I don't make the things on my list, I begin to feel a sense that I am losing something.
The memory of Tata Régine splattered with tomato juice making her coulis becomes
a little more distant. The taste of Papé Xime's olives fades in my mind. For all of us,
shown once how to make tablet, sloe gin, or vin d'orange by a dear friend, mother, or
grandfather, it becomes a small, life-affirming ritual. The tasks take on an important
if bittersweet meaning: the passing of yet another year, the work that we do in the
world, and the things that we must continue to grow, eat, and save.

les vendanges

Autumn is anchored in Provence by that most illustrious of fruit harvests: the grape harvest, known as *les vendanges*. Growing up, the vendanges were talked about in almost mythical terms and it was only as an adult that I began to help the family: children are spared the work, of course.

As September arrives Papé Xime will take a final walk through his vines, inspecting the heavy purple bunches. He will have a little nibble and say, *"Le vin sera excellent cette année."* He says this every year. Sample grapes are collected and driven to the cooperative cave to have their sugar levels tested. The ripeness and quantity of sugar in the grapes will determine the alcoholic strength of the wine made from them. If there is enough to reach 13.5 percent, then we're off, and the *vendanges* can begin.

Electric energy fills the air. The vineyards come alive with activity and people. Tractors whizz around in all directions from vineyards to the caves where they tip trailers, replete with grapes, straight into de-stemmers before speeding back to the fields where little sun hats bob up and down the rows of vines. Extended families and teams of hired pickers move in unison, harvesting bunches impossibly fast, filling up buckets, tipping their contents into a trailer, pulled by a tractor, which in turn moves with the pickers. It's an industrious yet festive atmosphere and we work in the knowledge that we are all a part of something bigger, that in farming communities across Europe, the same thing is happening.

In our family vineyards, we meet at eight thirty am. Papé always drives the tractor while the rest of us, his children and grandchildren, do the picking. Picking is a balance between going as fast as possible, keeping up with everyone, not missing a single bunch, and finding time to examine the grapes quickly, clipping off any that are rotten, unripe, or dried up, all of which would affect the quality of the wine. Sometimes you can see where a wild boar has had a bite. This doesn't matter, those go in too. My great-aunt also loves to eat grapes as she picks. Whenever I offer her water she will shake her head and say, *"J'ai mangé du raisin."*

We stop at midday to eat together, either picnicking in the shade of a *cabanon*, the little stone houses that dot the landscape or, if it's too hot, we will drive back to whichever family member owns the nearest farmhouse. On the menu will be Salade Composée (see page 122) with bread, followed by quiche (see page 37), then something roasted, then cheese, wine, and dessert.

On the last day of picking, we will have a big celebration lunch, *les grillades* (see page 102), in the vines: Serge's eggplant caviar on baguette to start, followed by green salad, and grilled merguez and lamb chops, and, of course, wine, toasting another year and another harvest.

Le vin

I won't get technical here since this could be
a book in itself, but I must mention the wine.
My family presently grows Grenache, Syrah
(Shiraz), Viognier, and clairette grapes for wine
making and muscat, cardinal, Italia, and prima
for eating.

We've been commercial *viticulteurs* since the
early 20th century when my great-grandfather,
Aimé Rimbert, saw the industry's lucrative
potential and co-founded the village's
cooperative cave with a few neighbors and
cousins. Prior to this, the grapes the family
grew were to make wine for household consumption. Our cousin Yannick still does this. The
cooperative cave was then named Les Roches Blanches, after the white rocks atop Mont Ventoux,
and today it is called Terraventoux.

For those who own chateaux and have the means to bottle and make the wine themselves, good
for them. For the rest of us, there's the cooperative cave. Cooperative wine is not a mishmash of
every grape brought by Tom, Dick, and Harry to the cave. The wines are expertly and beautifully
curated by outstanding oenologists, and the grapes and vineyards are grouped according to their
terroir and the subtle flavor this imparts to the wine.

My dad, Richard, now looks after the precious Grenache and Syrah vines for the *cavée* wine, vines
over 40 years old, which don't produce very much, but are among only a handful of vineyards that
contribute the grapes for this, our most exquisite wine.

Provence has a glamorous reputation, but for us, it is a place to work and to live as best as we can. I
have seen the hard side of farming here, the fickleness of nature. My dad and Papé Xime work all
year, but there comes a point when there isn't much to do but wait and hope. The same vineyard
could give two and a half tons of grapes one year and four hundred kilos (about 880 pounds) the
next. In spite of the slog, being an *agriculteur* is a privilege and there is something utterly joyful
about drinking the beautiful wines containing our grapes every year: La Cavée, Terre de Truffes,
Le Rosé.

toasted almonds

Almond trees blossom early in the New Year, in the dead of winter, and the fruit is picked at the height of summer. Our family production isn't commercial by any means. We pick those we can reach and those we can't we knock off with long sticks to fall on the ground. The best way to eat them is raw, as nature intended, but toasted and lightly salted, as my great-uncle Tonton Jo did in vast quantities after his own harvest, they make a perfect savory apéritif nibble. Tonton Jo would soak them before roasting, but I find this an unnecessary step.

Apéritif snacks are very much a thing in France and home drinks cabinets are stuffed to the brim with assorted packets of cheesy crackers, peanut-flavored chips, and other gloriously odd-shaped store-bought nibbles. It's always rather nice to have something homemade, too though. When I'm having people over on weeknights, a bowl of toasted, salted almonds on the table and a negroni cocktail thrust in friends' hands as they step in the door amount to borrowed time for me to finish clattering around the kitchen.

Serves 8,

as an apéritif nibble

2¾ cups (14 oz/400 g) raw shelled almonds

1 teaspoon sea salt

½ teaspoon paprika or piment d'espelette

2 teaspoons olive oil

Preheat the oven to 320°F (160°C). Lay the almonds on a baking pan and bake for 25–30 minutes. Keep an eye on them since oven temperatures do vary. Pound the salt to a fine powder in a mortar and mix with the paprika.

After the almonds have toasted, drizzle with the olive oil and sprinkle with the prepared salt and paprika. Shake the pan to coat evenly, then return to the oven for a further 5 minutes. Remove from the oven and cool before storing in an airtight container or placing in bowls and eating. They will keep in a sealed container for a few weeks.

tapenade

A sip of chilled rosé and a bite of toasted baguette smothered in tapenade is a fine way to start a meal. Sublimely rustic, this olive spread is versatile: spread on tartines (see below), smooth over a leg of lamb with a few extra anchovies before roasting, stir into pasta with basil and cherry tomatoes, whisk into omelets…

The name comes from the Provençal word for capers, tapèno.

Serves 6

7 oz (200 g) pitted black or green olives (drained weight)

1 garlic clove, crushed

1 heaped tablespoon capers

3 anchovy fillets

squeeze of lemon juice

1 teaspoon cognac

1 tablespoon olive oil

pinch of freshly ground black pepper

Place the olives in a large mortar. Add the garlic, then the capers and anchovy fillets. Pound and mash the ingredients until you have a paste, keeping a few visible bits of olive skin for texture. Add the lemon juice, cognac, and olive oil, and season with the black pepper. Store in the fridge until needed.

If you don't own a large mortar and pestle, place the ingredients in a bowl and use a handheld immersion blender to purée the dip. Ensure it is pulsed for just a few seconds at a time to keep some texture in the tapenade.

tartines

These toasts keep for a considerable amount of time. Made even weeks in advance, come their stage-call they will be delicious and crispy, perfect vessels for varied canapé toppings and dips. One 22 in (56 cm) baguette makes about 35 tartines, which is more than enough to serve with a bowl of tapenade, brandade, or hummus. Stale or fresh baguettes work just as well to make these: the bread just needs to be sliceable.

Makes about 35 tartines,
6–8 servings, depending on the size of your baguette

1 baguette

about 3 tablespoons olive oil

Preheat the oven to 400°F (200°C) and slice the baguette into ½ inch (1 cm) thick rounds. Lay the slices on a baking sheet and place the olive oil in a ramekin. Brush both sides of the slices with the olive oil using a pastry brush. Place the pan in the oven and bake for about 10 minutes, until golden brown. Place the tartines on a wire rack to cool, then store in an airtight container until needed.

salade composée

By the Basilique Saint Pierre in Avignon is a little restaurant where one can find the most beautiful salades composées: huge plates piled with impossibly high layers of oak leaf lettuce, hot goat cheese and thyme-encrusted tartines, perfectly ripe melon segments, the best local olives and tomatoes, cured ham, and toasted walnuts. None of it makes sense, but the elements work in harmony to form a delectable whole. That is what a salade composée should be.

Get invited to anyone's house in the south of France for lunch and your first course will either be a green salad or, indeed, a salade composée, whatever the time of year. The version here is a kind of Niçoise, the cooked paired with the raw: boiled beans and potatoes, together with the last of summer's tomato offering and some anchovies and eggs thrown in for good measure. Using potatoes, green beans, and eggs as a base, you could add extras according to availability: fresh fava beans, cooked artichoke hearts, or sliced radishes. Compose your own salad.

Serves 6,

as a first course

For the salad

2¼ lb (1 kg) waxy potatoes

10½ oz (300 g) green beans, trimmed

6 eggs

2 large ripe tomatoes, sliced

½ large white or red onion, finely sliced

2½ oz (70 g) black olives

¼ cup (⅓ oz/10 g) finely chopped parsley

12 anchovies (optional)

salt

For the dressing

big pinch of salt

1 tablespoon red wine vinegar

½ teaspoon freshly ground black pepper

5 tablespoons olive oil

1 heaped teaspoon Dijon mustard

For the salad, peel the potatoes and chop them into walnut-sized pieces. Place the potatoes in a large pan of fresh water with a big pinch of salt and bring to a boil. Boil for about 10 minutes, then add the green beans to the same pan and boil together for a further 8 minutes. Once all the vegetables are tender, drain and place in a colander to cool.

Meanwhile, bring a separate pan of water to a boil. Once the water is bubbling, carefully lower in the eggs and cook for 7–8 minutes, depending on their size. Then drain and allow to cool. Once cool, peel and halve, then set aside.

Prepare the salad dressing: add the salt and vinegar to a large salad bowl and whisk with a fork to dissolve. Follow with the black pepper, olive oil, and mustard and whisk again.

Add all of the salad ingredients, apart from the eggs and anchovies, to the salad bowl. Gently toss, then taste to check the seasoning, adding more salt if necessary. Once happy, top the salad with the eggs, along with the anchovies, if using. Place in the fridge or keep at room temperature until you are ready to serve.

crespéou

Serves 4

For the red omelet

2 tablespoons sunflower oil

½ red pepper, deseeded and finely chopped

1 shallot, finely chopped

3 eggs

1 tablespoon tomato paste

salt and freshly ground black pepper

For the plain omelet

3 eggs

pinch of freshly ground black pepper

2 tablespoons grated Emmental or Cheddar

1 tablespoon sunflower oil

For the black omelet

3 eggs

2 tablespoons black olive Tapenade (see page 120)

1 tablespoon sunflower oil

For the green omelet

3 eggs

4 sprigs of parsley, finely chopped

salt and freshly ground black pepper

1 tablespoon sunflower oil

Crespéou is made of different flavored omelets, piled on top of each other like a savory layer cake, generally served cool or at room temperature. A small frying pan or, ideally, an omelet pan is needed to make this. Omelet pans are a kitchen staple in France, thin and light, and with proper care they can last forever. Dish washing liquid shouldn't be used on them: they must be wiped clean, rinsed with water, then dried immediately.

Begin with the red omelet since it will take the longest. Place a small frying pan over medium heat and add 1 tablespoon of the sunflower oil. Add the red pepper and shallot and fry for 10 minutes, then remove from the heat and sprinkle with salt and black pepper. Crack the eggs into a mixing bowl, whisk in the tomato paste, and then add the red pepper and shallot, whisking until combined.

Preheat your broiler to high. Add the remaining sunflower oil to a small frying or omelet pan and place over medium–high heat on the stovetop. (If using the pan you used to cook the shallot and red pepper, ensure it is first wiped clean.) Pour in the red omelet mixture and cook for 1–2 minutes, using a spatula to coax the sides in a little, and lifting and inclining the pan to ensure the mixture gets well distributed. Finish the omelet under the broiler to cook the top, then carefully turn out onto a serving plate. Wipe any residual omelet off the pan, then begin the next.

To make the plain omelet, rinse the bowl used to whisk the red omelet mixture, then crack the eggs into it. Sprinkle in the black pepper and grated cheese, then whisk. Repeat the previous steps: frying in the sunflower oil, then finishing the omelet under the broiler, then turning it out on top of the red omelet.

For the black omelet, crack the eggs into the rinsed bowl and whisk in the tapenade. Fry as before, then turn out on top of the plain omelet. For the green omelet, crack the eggs into the bowl, add the parsley, and season with plenty of salt and black pepper. Fry as before, then assess which side is prettiest before turning nice-side up on top of the omelets. The crespéou can be sliced like a cake and served immediately or covered with foil and kept in the fridge once cooled.

petit épeautre et ses legumes

small spelt and vegetables

Long before grapes, long before olives, petit épeautre, aka einkorn wheat or small spelt, was grown and eaten in Provence. Well-adapted to the poor soil of the Haute Provence, it has seen a resurgence in popularity in the past 30 years thanks to a group of farmers near the town of Sault, who have dedicated themselves to protecting and reviving this 10,000-year-old species. The grain is not ideal for bread since it has a low gluten content, but left intact, the grains lend themselves perfectly to salads, soups, and stews and are a Provençal menu staple.

This dish is my favorite way of enjoying petit épeautre, simmered alongside a few companion vegetables in the pot. Once cooked, the grains are drained, the companion vegetables delicately sliced, and everything is covered in dressing with an extra few fresh vegetables tossed in. It's delicious, somehow buttery-tasting, and homey.

Einkorn wheat, or small spelt, can be difficult to find in grain form in many countries at the time of writing, but given the general renewed interest in heritage and alternative grains, I am hopeful that it is only a matter of time before it's easier to track down. In the meantime, one can substitute with spelt or barley.

Serves 4

1¼ cups (9 oz/250 g) einkorn wheat berries (small spelt)

2 carrots

1 leek

1 celery stick

2 shallots

generous squeeze of lemon juice

2 tablespoons red wine vinegar

3½ tablespoons olive oil

½ garlic clove, crushed

4 ripe tomatoes

salt and freshly ground black pepper

Place the einkorn in a bowl of tepid water to soak while you prepare the vegetables.

Peel and trim the carrots. Wash and trim the leek and celery, and peel and halve the shallots. Drain the soaked grains, place in a saucepan with the prepared vegetables, and cover with plenty of fresh water and a pinch of salt. Bring to a boil, then lower the heat and simmer for 20 minutes while you prepare your dressing.

In a serving bowl, whisk together the lemon juice, vinegar, and a generous pinch of salt. Once the salt has dissolved, add some black pepper and the olive oil and garlic.

Once the simmering grains and vegetables are tender, drain in a colander. Remove and slice the cooked vegetables, along with the tomatoes. Add the grains, sliced vegetables, and tomatoes to the bowl with the prepared dressing and toss immediately. Taste to check the seasoning and serve: this is delicious warm or at room temperature, if you wanted to prepare it in advance for a packed lunch.

escarole

Escarole with anchoïade dressing, an intense, chewy salad we most often eat in the colder months, is my dad's desert island dish, and I can see why. It is served with hot, fluffy boiled potatoes on the side to be crushed and enjoyed with the leaves, dressed in their piquant garlic and anchovy coating. My dad is absurdly particular about this dish, peering over the shoulder of anyone making it. "You're not chopping the celery finely enough," is the chief concern. Next comes, "more garlic" or, "You're overcooking the anchovies." His instructions are below, but thankfully you will be spared his running commentary in your kitchens.

Experiment and substitute the escarole for frisée, puntarelle, radicchio, or foraged dandelion greens (or even Romaine lettuce if you dislike bitter leaves). As a rule, the paler the leaves, the sweeter they will be. I occasionally buy two escarole heads for this reason when making this salad, removing all the outer darker leaves and using just the pale, yellow hearts. If you have a whole head of celery, cut from the very bottom of the white heart and add a few sliced fronds from the top for this element of the salad. Ensure it is chopped very finely, since its primary role here is to contribute a subtle, sweet aniseed flavor rather than large crunchy, stringy celery chunks. Serve this as a substantial autumn appetizer for four, to be followed by roast lamb or perhaps some poached salmon.

Serves 4

14 oz (400 g) potatoes

4 anchovies

4–5 tablespoons olive oil

1½ tablespoons red wine vinegar

squeeze (less than 1 tablespoon) lemon juice

½ teaspoon freshly ground black pepper, plus extra to serve

1 large garlic clove, crushed

1¾ oz (50 g) celery, fronds and heart (approx. 4 inches/10 cm), very finely chopped

1 head escarole, washed and dried (approx. 12 oz/350 g)

salt

Wash and peel the potatoes. Chop into even chunks the size of walnuts and place in a saucepan of fresh water. Bring to a boil, then lower the heat and fast-simmer for 15 minutes, until the potatoes are tender. Drain and set aside.

While the potatoes are cooking, prepare the dressing. Place the anchovies in a small saucepan and cover with 1 tablespoon of the olive oil. Place over the lowest heat and stir with a wooden spoon for 1–2 minutes, until the anchovies have dissolved into a brown paste. If your lowest setting is still quite hot, lift and hover the pan above the heat to achieve this brown anchovy paste without any overcooking. Once ready, remove from the heat immediately.

Add the red wine vinegar to a large salad bowl, followed by the dissolved anchovies, the remaining 3–4 tablespoons of the olive oil, and the lemon juice and black pepper. Add the garlic, then whisk the dressing. Taste to check the seasoning, adjusting if necessary. More olive oil is never a bad idea.

Place the celery in the salad bowl on top of the dressing, along with the washed and dried escarole.

Now the dish is ready to eat: place a few warm potatoes onto each plate, grind over some black pepper, and sprinkle with salt. Toss the salad, then serve immediately alongside the potatoes.

roasted autumn veggies

Butternut squash does not need to be peeled when it is being roasted, since the skin will get deliciously soft and just a little chewy. We grow butternut squash and musquée de Provence very successfully in our garden here in Provence, and this dish is one to which we often turn.

Serves 4

1 butternut squash, seeds and stringy flesh removed, then sliced into ¾ inch (2 cm) segments

3 carrots, peeled and halved lengthways

3 sage leaves

3 bay leaves

3 garlic cloves, lightly bashed in their skins

big pinch of coarse sea salt

1 teaspoon freshly ground black pepper

¼ cup (60 ml) olive oil, plus extra to serve

2¾ cups (1 lb/450 g) drained cooked chickpeas (2 x 14 oz/400 g cans)

5½ oz (150 g) feta

1 heaped tablespoon pumpkin seeds

½ lemon

Preheat the oven to 400°F (200°C). Distribute the squash on a large baking pan. Add the carrots to the pan, along with the sage and bay leaves, and the garlic cloves. Sprinkle with the coarse sea salt and black pepper, then drizzle over the olive oil. Place the pan in the oven and roast for about 45 minutes, until the vegetables are soft and brown in places.

Place the chickpeas in a large serving bowl. Add the roasted vegetables, discarding the bay leaves, but crumbling in at least one of the sage leaves (or more depending on their size and pungency). Squeeze the garlic cloves out of their skins and add. Crumble over the feta and add the pumpkin seeds.

Toss and add an extra few tablespoons of olive oil and a squeeze or two of lemon juice to taste. Enjoy warm or at room temperature.

soupe de moules

When World War II broke out, my great-grandmother Antoinette bought a cow. She knew hard times were on their way and, while her husband, Aimé, went off to fight, she ran the big farm herself. During the occupation, the people staying at La Cointe could include the extended family, farm hands, seasonal pickers, visitors, *réfractaires,* and fellow *résistants.* "I spent the war cooking for the masses and washing sheets," Mamé would say, and I can see her point. There was a constant stream of people to cook and cater for and to look after. The family was very grateful for the cow, the milk, and thus the butter and cheese she provided, but after the war, Mamé was thrilled to be able to vary the family diet again, and in particular get ahold of seafood. She made a lot of soupe de moules, her daughter Edmée tells me, and grilled scallops.

What is good about this soup is that a bag of mussels goes a very long way: the mussels are cooked separately, and their cooking liquor is added to the simmering soup, imparting their incredible flavor to it. The trick is to never boil this soup, so consider that the pasta will take longer than usual to cook.

Serves 4,
as a main course

2 lb 10 oz (1.2 kg) mussels in
their shells

1 cup (250 ml) dry white wine

3 tablespoons olive oil

6 small shallots, finely chopped

1 large carrot, finely chopped

1 celery stick, finely chopped

1 large leek, sliced into ½ inch
(1 cm) rounds

½ teaspoon fennel seeds,
crushed using a mortar and
pestle

2 sprigs of thyme

3 bay leaves

3 tomatoes

2½ cups (600 ml) fish stock
(fresh or from a bouillon cube)

1 garlic clove, finely sliced

scant ½ cup (2½ oz/70 g) orzo
(or other small pasta)

freshly ground black pepper

1–2 quantities of Garlic
Croutons (see page 199),
to serve (optional)

Place the mussels in a sink filled with fresh water. Pick them up
one by one and, using a knife, pull off the beards. Scrape away
any barnacles growing on the outside of the shell. If any shells are
cracked or won't shut when tapped or pressed, discard. Place the
prepared mussels in a bowl of fresh water.

Place a large pot over high heat and pour in the white wine. Once
bubbling, add the drained mussels and cover the pot. Steam,
shaking the pot a little, for 2 minutes, until the shells have opened.
Turn the heat off and use a slotted spoon to lift the mussels out
of the pot and into a bowl. Discard any that haven't opened. The
delicious liquid remaining in the pot will be added to your soup at
a later stage, but it must be left to settle to avoid any grit or sand the
mussels may have given off making it into your soup: pour into a
clear mixing bowl and set aside.

Now begin the soup. Add the olive oil to a large pot over medium–
low heat (I rinse the large pot I cooked the mussels in and use this
to cook the soup). Add the vegetables and crushed fennel seeds,
followed by the thyme and bay leaves. Soften the vegetables for 20
minutes without browning. Stir and put the lid on from time to
time to encourage them to steam in their own juices.

While the vegetables are cooking, remove all but a handful of
mussels from their shells (I keep a few intact for aesthetic reasons).
Peel the tomatoes by immersing them in boiling water for 1 minute,
then peeling off the skins. Roughly chop the peeled tomatoes.
Prepare the fish stock, reheating it if fresh, or dissolving a bouillon
cube in boiling water if not.

Once the vegetables in the pot are nicely softened and cooked, add
the chopped tomatoes, garlic, and some black pepper to the pot.
Resist the temptation to add salt. Reduce the tomatoes for a few
minutes, then add the reserved mussel cooking liquid, pouring it
in carefully and avoiding adding the last few tablespoons at the
bottom of the mixing bowl, lest there be any grit. Add half of the
stock and gently simmer the soup for 10 minutes to develop the
flavors, then add the pasta.

While the pasta is cooking, (which will take longer than usual since
the soup broth should not be boiling), quickly prepare some garlic
croutons, if you wish. Once the pasta is cooked, assess the amount
of liquid and top up with the remaining fish stock, if necessary.
Once happy, return all of the mussels to the pot. Simmer together
for 1 minute, then serve immediately in bowls, and top with the
garlic croutons, if using.

squash soup

I have had to restrain myself from filling this book with vegetable soup recipes, aware that not everybody shares my monomania. Though it is worth noting that the English word "supper" finds its origins in the French *souper*, designating it an evening meal typically composed of bread and a vegetable or meat broth.

We eat a lot of soup in Provence and it is much more than a case of just using up vegetables. *La soupe* is one of the pillars of French home cooking: humble, dignified, economical. A vast steaming pot on the table a reassuring presence in our warm homes after rich lunches or long days at work in the colder months.

Once a soup has been ladled into bowls, diners should customize their own—or not—according to their fancy. Croutons (see page 199), lemon juice, olive oil, Gruyère, Cheddar, bread, crème fraîche and a pat of butter are all excellent additions to soups, though perhaps not all together.

Serves 4–6

4¼ cups (1 liter) chicken stock

2 tablespoons (1 oz/30 g) butter

2 onions, roughly chopped

2 carrots, peeled and roughly chopped

1 celery stick, roughly chopped

1 Parmesan rind

1 butternut squash, or ¼ musquée de Provence, peeled, deseeded, and chopped into chunks

1 potato, peeled and chopped

½ teaspoon piment d'espelette or cayenne pepper

olive oil

juice of ½ lemon

salt and freshly ground black pepper

Warm the stock and prepare your vegetables, then boil a kettle of water.

Place a large Dutch oven or soup pot over medium–low heat and add the butter. Once melted, add the onions, carrots, celery, and the Parmesan rind. Soften for 15 minutes, stirring every so often, then add the chopped squash and potato, along with the espelette or cayenne pepper.

Increase the heat and continue to stir for a few minutes, adding some olive oil if necessary, then pour the warmed chicken stock into the pan, followed by about 2 cups (500 ml) of hot water from the kettle.

Liberally add salt and black pepper, then bring the soup to a boil. Lower the heat and simmer for 30 minutes, covered, until all the vegetables are tender. Remove the Parmesan rind and discard. Add 3 tablespoons of olive oil and the lemon juice. Using a handheld immersion blender, purée the soup, then serve immediately.

pot-au-feu

I didn't make pot-au-feu for years, convinced it was expensive, that one needed lots of different types of meat… This is not true, and one can make a pot-au-feu from a single large piece of stewing beef. If purchasing the meat from a butcher, you may as well ask for some marrow bones, and perhaps a chopped oxtail to throw in, but going without these elements is not something to worry about. The only thing to bear in mind is that pre-cut chunks of stewing beef, as often found in stores, will not do: it must be whole, or at the very least in large pieces the size of hands.

When up or downscaling the recipe, for the vegetables ensure that every diner gets a little of everything, and put a few extra in for the pot. You could make pot-au-feu with just potatoes, carrots, and onions as the sides—it is supposed to be a cheap and cheerful dish after all—but a whole fennel bulb could also be a nice addition at the right time of year, or half a Savoy cabbage for those who don't mind how it flavors the broth. Some cooks will boil the potatoes separately to preserve the clarity of the broth, but I think it's just easier to embrace the convenience and aspect of this as a one-pot dish.

Serves 6–8

3 lb 5 oz (1.2–1.5 kg) beef (such as brisket, ox cheeks, forequarter flank, or top rump)

1 oxtail, chopped (optional)

1–2 marrow bones, chopped (optional)

1 onion, peeled

5 cloves

6 peppercorns

3 juniper berries

4 sprigs of parsley

4 sage leaves

1 rosemary sprig

3 sprigs of thyme

3 bay leaves

1 star anise

8 carrots

3 leeks

Cont'd overleaf.

Place the beef in the largest stock pot or Dutch oven you have. Add the oxtail, if using, but not the marrow bones (these are added later with the vegetables). Stud the onion with the cloves. Add this to the pot, along with the peppercorns and juniper berries. Add the parsley, sage, rosemary, thyme, bay leaves, and star anise. Cover the beef, onion, and aromatics with 17 cups (4 liters) of water, cover the pot, and place over low heat. Slowly bring to a simmer: it is normal for this to take 45 minutes or more. Simmer, covered, for 4 hours. After the first hour or so, lift the lid from time to time and use a slotted spoon to skim off any scum that forms on the surface.

While the beef is simmering, prepare the vegetables. Trim and peel the carrots but leave them whole. Trim and wash the leeks and leave whole if the size of your pot allows it. Peel the potatoes and halve if on the large side. Trim and wash the celery. Trim and peel the turnips.

After the beef has simmered for 4 hours, add the vegetables and marrow bones to the pot. Replace the lid and simmer for a further 1 hour, until the vegetables are very tender. There should be no hint of crunch when eating pot-au-feu vegetables.

When the pot-au-feu is ready to serve, place the cornichons, mustards, and ketchup on the table. Turn the heat off under the pot and place a sieve over a large mixing bowl. Drain the vegetables, meat, and bones, setting the broth aside.

8 potatoes

2 celery sticks

8 turnips

To serve

cornichons

whole-grain mustard

Dijon mustard

ketchup

Discarding any remaining aromatics, such as the cloves from the onion and any loose herbs or spices, slice the vegetables and meat into manageable pieces, and arrange with the marrow bones and oxtail pieces (if using) on a serving platter. Bring the platter to the table and allow diners to help themselves to a few pieces of every element. Pot-au-feu is also delicious as a cold buffet.

Using the Pot-au-Feu Broth

The broth should be set aside and, once cooled, the layer of fat skimmed off the top. The broth can be reheated and served with crusty bread and olive oil as with the One Soup, Two Courses (see page 158). Some small pasta and crushed garlic could be added to it as with the Aïgo Boulido (see page 33).

fennel in white wine

Here fennel is braised with white wine, tomatoes, and lardons until completely tender: excellent as a hot appetizer, or as part of a main course alongside some rice or grilled fish. For a vegetarian version, replace the lardons with a handful of olives or, simply, more red pepper flakes. In springtime, consider swapping the fennel for 6–8 halved endives and omit the tomatoes.

Serves 4

2 tablespoons olive oil

2 onions, roughly chopped

2 bay leaves

1 teaspoon dried thyme

3½ oz (100 g) smoked lardons

3 fennel bulbs, trimmed, halved, then sliced into three

pinch of red pepper flakes

1¼ cups (300 ml) white wine

14 oz (400 g) can of whole plum tomatoes

salt and freshly ground black pepper

Place a large sauté pan or Dutch oven over medium heat and drizzle in the olive oil. Add the chopped onions, bay leaves, thyme, and lardons, then fry for 8 minutes, stirring frequently. Add the fennel to the pan, then, stirring frequently, sauté for about 5 minutes to coat in the oil and juices. After this stage, add the red pepper flakes, pour in the white wine, and allow to bubble for 1–2 minutes, then stir in the can of tomatoes, some salt, and plenty of black pepper. Cover the pan, lower the heat, and then braise for 45 minutes to 1 hour, turning the fennel pieces every so often until tender. Serve hot.

épaule d'agneau a la Provençale

shoulder of lamb on fondant potatoes

There is something wonderful about having friends over when the weather is miserable outside: it is permissible to sit indoors over a long lunch, fuelled by wine, whisky, and a delicious roast. For this Provençal classic, everything is cooked together in one pan: a herb-encrusted shoulder of lamb sits on a bed of potatoes and tomatoes, generously giving its juices and incredible flavor to them as it roasts. The potatoes also sit in half an inch of stock, rendering their bottoms melt-in-the-mouth while their tops crisp up beautifully.

Serves 6

For the lamb

3½–4½ lb (1.6–2 kg) lamb shoulder

3 tablespoons olive oil

3 sprigs of rosemary, leaves picked and finely chopped

1 heaped teaspoon dried thyme

sea salt flakes and freshly ground black pepper

For the potatoes

3 lb 5 oz (1.5 kg) potatoes, cut into 1 inch (2.5 cm) chunks

14 oz (400 g) ripe tomatoes

5 bay leaves

4 garlic cloves, lightly bashed in their skins

1 heaped teaspoon dried thyme

extra virgin olive oil

2 cups (450 ml) vegetable or chicken stock

Remove the lamb shoulder from the fridge at least 2 hours before it is to be roasted. Preheat the oven to 425°F (220°C).

Pour 1 tablespoon of the olive oil over the base of a relatively deep roasting pan or large lasagne dish. Arrange the potatoes in the dish. Chop the tomatoes into similar-sized pieces and add to the potatoes. Add the bay leaves and garlic cloves. Sprinkle over the thyme and plenty of salt and black pepper, followed by a few tablespoons of extra virgin olive oil. Mix together, then pour in two-thirds of the stock, aiming for the liquid to come halfway up the potatoes.

Place the lamb shoulder directly on the potatoes and drizzle over the olive oil. Sprinkle over the rosemary, along with the thyme, and season with salt and freshly ground black pepper.

Pop the dish in the oven. Roast for 1 hour 10 minutes to 1½ hours, depending on the size of your shoulder. Turn the meat over every 30 minutes and keep an eye on the level of liquid in the base: if it ever looks too dry, pour in the remaining stock. After 1½ hours, your shoulder should be ready and hopefully still nice and pink in the center. Remove the dish from the oven and place the meat on a board to rest, covered in foil.

Assess the potatoes: those that have been sitting directly under the meat may lack that desirable golden brown crispy top. If this is the case, turn the oven up to 475°F (240°C) while the meat is resting on the counter, and put the potatoes back in for 5–10 minutes to cook to perfection.

Carve the rested meat and serve together with the potatoes and copious amounts of red wine.

lapin d'automne

autumn rabbit

The crack of a rifle shot echoing through the countryside heralds the end of summer for all, and the beginning of game hunting season for some. Hunters, *les chasseurs*, have an understanding with farmers: they may roam the land, seeking wild rabbit, hare, and deer throughout the season, provided they pick up the bullet cartridges that drop to the ground after every shot. There isn't much of a hunting tradition in my family. Wildlife is seen as something to treasure, something to observe, but we have a no-nonsense attitude to rearing animals at home for food. Namely fancy-feathered chickens and rabbits.

Rabbit stew was a family staple growing up: rich without being fatty, autumnal, cozy. This recipe embodies all of this, and is my definitive dinner party dish in the colder months. It is a dinner party dish because I think of rabbit as special. Serve it with a generous pile of buttery mashed potatoes and steamed lacinato kale. I suggest using 4½ lb (2 kg) potatoes for eight people.

Rabbit is often available from butchers, but call them in advance to check, and expect to have to wait a day or two for them to source it if they do not have any. Wild rabbits are smaller, and if this is what your butcher is providing, you may need three. Alternatively, substitute the rabbit in this recipe for guinea fowl or chicken, supplemented with a couple of extra chicken thighs if you are worried about quantities or love leftovers as much as I do.

Serves 6–8

2 rabbits, cut into joints
(approx. 3½ lb/1.6 kg in total)

2 onions, roughly chopped

1 large head of garlic, cloves
peeled

3 bay leaves

2 sprigs of thyme

2 cups (3 oz/80 g) fresh parsley,
roughly chopped

14 oz (400 g) smoked lardons

750 ml bottle of full-bodied red
wine

1 cup (250 ml) red wine
vinegar

5 tablespoons olive oil,
plus extra if needed

2 tablespoons tomato paste

Place the rabbit pieces in a large, non-metallic bowl and stir in the onions, garlic, bay leaves, thyme, parsley, lardons, red wine, and vinegar. Cover and leave to marinate in the fridge for 4 hours.

Place a large Dutch oven or heavy-bottomed pot over medium heat and heat the olive oil. Using tongs, pick up the pieces of rabbit, allowing any excess marinade to run off back into the bowl, and add to the pot. Brown the meat in batches, setting each batch aside as you go and adding more olive oil to the pan when necessary. Once you have finished, strain the marinade so you are left with the garlic, onions, herbs, and lardons (reserve the liquid —you'll add it back in later) and add them to the pan you used to cook the rabbit, along with more olive oil, if needed.

Once the onions and lardons are cooked (your kitchen will be smelling delicious at this point), add the meat back to the pot, in layers if necessary, followed by the marinade liquid and the tomato paste. Bring to a simmer and cook for 1 hour, with the pan partially covered.

The dish is now ready and the meat should be nice and tender. You can either leave it to rest for a few hours and reheat, or keep it covered and warm until you are ready to serve.

Suggestion for using up leftovers in Rabbit Pappardelle

You only need one or two portions of rabbit and a few tablespoons of leftover sauce to make a delicious pasta dish for two from the leftovers. Carefully pull any leftover meat off the bones, then shred or finely slice. Discard the bones and place the prepared meat back into the sauce. Add a pat of butter and heat.

Meanwhile, bring a pan of salted water to a boil and cook 3½ oz (100 g) of pasta per person. Drain the pasta, then stir into sauce. Add an extra pat of butter and some black pepper, and serve immediately with Parmesan and perhaps a green salad on the side.

apple compote

This is probably a record, a cookbook recipe containing only one ingredient. Yet this is what is beautiful about apples: cooked in their own juices and then puréed, they form a simple yet fragrant compote, one my mom has been making for as long as I can remember. Add cinnamon or perhaps vanilla seeds if desired, but organic sweet apples really will be perfect just as they are.

The quantity of apples below makes a relatively big batch because the resulting compote has two destinies: half is to be enjoyed over the coming days at breakfast and teatime, and the remainder will be funneled into jars, then canned and stowed away, ready for a brunch, breakfast, or dessert, months down the line. If canning seems like too much of an effort (review the USDA Complete Guide to Home Canning for techniques), compote also keeps well in the freezer. Our freezer is always full of unidentified bags of "soups" that, on more than one occasion, have turned out to be compotes.

Makes approx. 8½ cups (2 liters)

6 lb 10 oz (3 kg) eating apples (15–18 apples, depending on their size) peeled, cored, quartered, then halved

Equipment:

3–5 sterilized pint-size (16 oz/500 ml) preserving jars

1 extra-large lidded pot (for canning)

Place the prepared apples in a large pot. Cover the pot and place over low heat. Allow the apples to gently steam in their own juices for about 45 minutes, keeping a close eye on them and stirring every so often, until they are tender. If you are concerned about the apples catching, add a few tablespoons of water. After 45 minutes, use a potato masher to crush them in the pan. Gently cook the mashed apples (there should be barely a wisp of a bubble) for a further 5–10 minutes, then follow-up with a handheld immersion blender or food processor for a silky-smooth finish.

While the apples are cooking, ready the jars. When the compote is ready, you might wish to pour half into a serving bowl to enjoy over the coming days (set it aside to cool, then cover and place the bowl in the fridge until use). Using a funnel, pour the remaining compote into the jars while it is still hot, leaving ¾ inch (2 cm) of headspace at the top of each jar. Cover with the lids.

Place a canning rack or clean dish towel in the bottom of your extra-large pot and add as many jars as will fit. Fill with enough hot water to cover the jars by at least 1 inch (2.5 cm). Cover with a lid and bring to a boil over medium heat. Once the water is boiling vigorously, set a timer for 1 hour.

After an hour, turn off the heat and leave the pot to cool slightly. Remove the jars and allow them to cool very slowly. Once cool, check the seals. If any of the jars haven't sealed, refrigerate and use immediately. Stick a label on the sealed jars indicating the year and the contents (an oft overlooked but important step), and store in a cool dark place: use within a year. Refrigerate after opening.

la panade

grated apple tart

In addition to bats and mice, the attic at the old farm was full of carefully stored apples that my grandfather and his siblings were sent up to fetch by Mamé Antoinette. These apples provided the basis for countless desserts in late autumn, winter, and early spring: tarte tatin; baked apples stuffed with butter, sugar, and spices; silky Compote (see page 143); and panade, a Provençal classic.

Uncomplicated to make, refreshingly un-faddy, yet impressive, panade is simply grated apples on a rich shortcrust pastry, baked until the pastry is crisp and the fruit becomes melt-in-the-mouth. If timing allows, it is delicious served warm with a scoop of vanilla ice cream. It can also be served as one of Les Treize Desserts (see page 190) at Christmas.

Serves 8

2⅓ cups (10½ oz/300 g) all-purpose flour, plus extra for rolling

pinch of salt

11 tablespoons (5½ oz/150 g) cold butter

½ cup (3½ oz/100 g) white sugar

1 egg, lightly beaten

1¾ lb (800 g) sweet apples

pinch of ground cinnamon

splash of milk

2 tablespoons turbinado or brown sugar

First prepare the pastry. Place the flour and salt in a mixing bowl and whisk together. Chop the butter into cubes and rub into the flour using your fingertips. When it has the texture of breadcrumbs, mix in the white sugar, followed by the beaten egg and 1 tablespoon of cold water. Keep adding water, a tablespoon at a time, combining and squeezing the mixture with your hands, until the pastry comes together into a ball (2 tablespoons of water usually suffice). Wrap the ball in plastic and chill in the fridge for 30 minutes.

While the pastry is chilling, thoroughly grease and line the base of an 11 inch (28 cm) loose-bottomed tart or quiche pan with parchment paper. Preheat the oven to 400°F (200°C).

Remove the pastry from the fridge and, using a lightly floured rolling pin, roll into a circle on a sheet of lightly floured parchment paper on a smooth surface. Continue rolling to enlarge the circle, sprinkling the surface of the pastry with flour for ease of rolling, until it is 3 inches (7.5 cm) wider than the pan on all sides.

Lifting up the pastry, parchment paper and all, gently flip it over into the pan, pushing it into postion. Discard the parchment paper. Firmly roll the rolling pin over the top edge of the pan, then pull away the excess pastry hanging over the edges. Prick the base of the tart all over with a fork and place in the fridge.

Re-roll the leftover pastry out on a lightly floured surface and cut into 7–10 strips, each 1 inch (2.5 cm) wide. You can use a pastry or pasta wheel to do this to create nice serrated edges. Place the strips in the fridge.

Peel and core the apples, then roughly grate them into a bowl. Sprinkle the cinnamon over the fruit and mix well. Remove the pastry-lined pan from the fridge and spoon the grated apples inside. Level the surface of the grated apples, then position the cut pastry strips over the top of the panade in a criss-cross pattern. If there is any overhang, trim the strips using the pastry wheel. Brush all visible pastry with the milk, then sprinkle over the turbinado or brown sugar.

Bake the tart in the oven for 55 minutes, or until the pastry is cooked. Remove from the oven, gently lift out of the tart pan, and place on a wire rack to cool. Enjoy the panade hot or at room temperature.

gâteau au yaourt

quince and yogurt cake

On the farm, however far away in the woods my cousins and I would be playing, come four o'clock we would march back to the house for some *goûter*: ordinarily a piece of fresh baguette stuffed with four squares of milk chocolate, but every so often, a slice of very simple cake such as this one, dunked in a glass of milk before each bite.

Gateau au yaourt is how I and millions of other French children over the past century were introduced to baking. A single-serving container of plain yogurt is tipped into a mixing bowl. The empty container is then used to measure the rest of the ingredients. Beautifully simple. Gateau au yaourt is a little denser than sponge cake and thus works well with a lovely hot drink like coffee.

Serves 6–8

1 quince peeled, cored, and sliced into ⅛ inch (5 mm) thick segments

1 single-serving container of plain yogurt (about ½ cup/ 4¼ oz/120 g)

1 container of sugar

pinch of salt

3 eggs

½ container of sunflower oil

zest of ½ lemon

1 teaspoon baking powder

3 containers of all-purpose flour

Place the quince in a small saucepan and cover with water. Place over medium heat and bring to a boil, then simmer for about 10 minutes, until the quince is tender. Remove from the heat.

Preheat the oven to 400°F (200°C). Grease and line the base of a 9 by 5½ inch (23 by 13 cm) loaf pan.

Pour the yogurt into a mixing bowl. Scrape every last bit of yogurt from the container, then fill the empty container with sugar and pour it into the bowl. Add the pinch of salt and mix well with a whisk. Crack in the eggs, then whisk to combine. Add the sunflower oil, lemon zest, and baking powder, then whisk again. Fill the empty yogurt container with flour and add to the bowl, repeat twice, then whisk it in.

Chop about half of the cooked quince slices into small pieces, about the size of raisins, then stir them into the batter. Pour the batter into your prepared pan, then arrange the remaining pieces of quince on top of the cake.

Bake for 45 minutes, though after about 30 minutes, cover the cake with foil to prevent the quince from blackening in places, if this is a concern.

Check the cake is cooked by pricking the center with a toothpick or sharp knife: if it comes out clean, the cake is ready, otherwise return it to the oven for a little longer.

Allow the cake to rest for a few minutes in the pan, then transfer to a wire rack. Once cool, place the cake on a serving plate or in a cake tin until you are ready to serve it with a pot of hot coffee.

"Vieille marmite, bonne soupe."

Provençal proverb

winter

WHEREVER WE LIVE, COME THE END OF THE YEAR, plates of walnuts, oranges, and clementines appear in our kitchens. Dining tables are covered with a confetti of citrus peelings and cracked nut shells after meals. I always watch, fascinated, as Papé Xime opens his walnuts like oysters for his dessert: he slips the tip of a sharp knife into the base of the nut where the two sides meet and twists. The shell opens and two perfect walnut halves come out every time.

There is no place like Provence in midwinter. The tourists have gone. The olive harvest is over. Everywhere is still and quiet and the smell of wood smoke in the air reminds us that, hopefully, a warm home awaits us somewhere.

When people think of Mediterranean cooking in general, summer dishes are often those that spring to mind: grilled fish, roasted tomatoes, eggplants… However, in my opinion, the very best Mediterranean flavors can be found in the winter salads, the frisée, the escarole, and the stews and ragouts, such as Wild Boar Civet (see page 171) and Daube (see page 173)… slow-cooked dishes I hope readers will come to enjoy cooking for loved ones. These dishes are also a real treat for intimate weeknight gatherings, provided they have been cooked the night before and reheated slowly the following day before serving: they often taste better for it.

olives

Olive trees are beautiful cultural and spiritual symbols, almost indestructible, and each with the potential to live for millennia. It's easy to forget this when planting an olive tree for its (undeniable) ornamental beauty and structure in backyards, as has become popular in recent years. In Provence, olive trees were traditionally planted by farmers in companion with vines to make oil for the household. When, after 60 years, vines generally have to be replanted, olive trees will just be beginning to show their full potential.

My family were subsistence farmers up until a century ago, but the way we produce our olive oil has not changed since those days. The olives are grown organically and the resulting pressed oil is for the extended family only. We might sell a little surplus, but as it is so precious, it can be hard to part with, even for a good price. My grandfather remembers when his dad, Aimé, lost many trees in the terrible frost of 1956, when temperatures suddenly descended to minus twenty degrees Celcius (minus four degrees Fahrenheit) overnight, causing catastrophic tree and plant losses across the Mediterranean. Overall, growing olives is relatively hands-off compared to viticulture, thus a joy for the busy grape farmer: a light prune in the spring and some manure, a few waterings in summer if it has not rained very much. It is the picking that takes the most time.

LES OLIVADES

We hand-pick the olives for oil in winter once they have turned from firm and green to slightly wrinkly and dark. The exact date we pick depends on various factors, but it is generally between November and December, since the later the harvest the riper the olive, and therefore the higher quantity of oil it will yield.

When it is time, Papé Xime first estimates the weight of our harvest by walking through the groves. I am always astonished at his accuracy, "*2300 kilos cette année*," because we don't pick anywhere near the same amount every year: it can oscillate between zero and two tons from one to the next.

Wrapped in our woollens and hats, we get to work in teams as an extended family, up three-footed ladders known as chevalets, using little rakes to brush the olives onto nets draped on the ground below. Pitching in and helping with each other's harvests speeds and livens up the process and whoever's olives we are picking that day has to provide lunch for all: the olive picker's picnic.

After a morning of working and gossiping with each other through the branches, the grove "host" calls a break: "*Allez on mange!*" We clamber out from the trees, empty olive crates are turned upside down and sat on, and we stop to eat from our laps. One olive picker's picnic fixed in my memory is the one my great-aunt and I shared when tackling three of her very large, very old trees awkwardly growing on an embankment. We sat down and shared a can of brandade de morue on baguette.

Some sliced couenne sausage with lentils, still warm from being cooked that morning, followed by some Comté (we are never without a cheese course, even when picnicking) on more baguette and, to finish, a cup of hot chicory from a thermos, with a few squares of dark chocolate. Heavenly.

In spite of the multiple lunch courses, we will generally only break for 30 minutes, then it's back to work until we lose the light. In an average year, the olives take thirty days to harvest from the first tree to the last. Though not as physically demanding as the vendanges, at the end of a day of picking olives in the middle of winter with a blowing mistral, our muscles are very stiff. A bath and a quiet evening in front of the fire is necessary.

NEW SEASON OLIVE OIL

Once the olives are picked and sorted (i.e. leaves, stalks, and twigs removed), we drive the olives in Papé Xime's truck to the cooperative mill at Malemort to be cold pressed. The yield for olive oil is approximately 20 percent, so for every 100 kilos (220 lb) of olives, we will get 20 liters (about 5¼ gallons) of olive oil or thereabouts. It is always very exciting every year to see the final process at the mill. The oil is given to us in 10 liter (2½ gallon) plastic containers, but we quickly decant it at home into glass bottles and store in the dark so it keeps well until the following harvest.

In Europe, fresh, new season olive oil should be sought out in food and farmers' markets between November and January. It will be perfect in simple salads and with baguette, however, newly pressed olive oil is also the traditional ingredient in Christmas Day's Pompe à Huile (see page 191). Aïoli, too, is wonderful with fresh garlic in the spring (see page 51) but is also a way to celebrate the new olive oil in winter.

Olive oil, like wine, is a snapshot of a year, of a terroir, of the variety of olive, but it will vary in flavor also depending on when the olives were harvested: picked earlier it can taste "greener," perhaps almost grassy; picked later it will have a smoother taste. As I have emphasized in the Provençal Larder (see pages 10–12), all olive oils are special as long as they have been grown with no chemical intervention and are cold pressed.

OLIVES FOR EATING

In Provence, every grove of, say, a hundred trees for oil will traditionally have one or two trees set aside with olives destined for eating, usually salonique or picholine varieties. Olives straight off the tree are inedible. Their inherent bitterness must be removed through a process involving salt, time, and aromatics. The length of time required to process and make an olive taste delicious will depend on the variety, but with a little nibble every so often, it will be easy to judge when they are at the perfect stage for eating. Here are the methods we use for preparing and brining delicious ripe black olives, for you to try should you have a tree in your backyard that produces some of a decent size. The tree may, of course, be an ornamental variety that doesn't produce perfectly ideal olives for eating, but since so little investment is required, it is definitely worth trying.

The dry salt-cure method

Wait until the olives turn purply-black and pick the loveliest from the tree. Pull off and discard any stalks and leaves. Prick each olive a few times with a fork, then place in a non-metallic bowl. Sprinkle over a handful or two of coarse sea salt (or more depending on the quantity of olives). Give the bowl a shake, then leave on the counter to dry-cure, tossing them a few times a day. After a week has passed, taste an olive. Add more salt if they still taste a little bitter at this stage. Wait a few more days, then eat another. As a general rule, after a few weeks, the olives can be eaten as they are, sprinkled with herbs, or stored in jars and covered with a brine to add more flavor. If the olives taste ready at any point but too salty, soak them in a cold bowl of water for a few hours before serving. If any mold appears at any point, add more salt.

To make the brine, heat 4¼ cups (1 liter) of water and add ⅓ cup (3½ oz/100 g) of salt, 2 bay leaves, and some wild fennel. Simmer until the salt has dissolved, cool, then pour over the olives in sterilized jars. Seal, then a week later, the olives should have taken on the aroma of the brine and will be ready to eat.

The water-cure method

Wait until the olives turn purply-black and pick the loveliest from the tree. Pull off and discard any stalks and leaves. Prick each olive a few times with a fork, then place them all in a bowl. Cover with cold water and ensure they are submerged by weighing them down with cans, if necessary. Soak for 7–10 days, changing the water every 24 hours. Taste an olive after 7 days and, if mild-tasting enough, they can all now be brined: drain the olives and place in sterilized preserving jars. Prepare a brine as above. Once cool, pour the brine over the olives in the jars. Seal the jars. A week later, the olives will have taken on the aroma of the brine and can be eaten.

winter salad

Cousin Anne and her husband Olivier live near Saint Remy de Provence, but on weekends return to work the land of which they are now custodians near our own. A host of good friends often join them when it is time to harvest their olives, honorary WWOOFERs (World Wide Opportunities on Organic Farms). Afterwards everyone gathers, eats, and sleeps at the old family farmhouse nearby, La Touraine.

La Touraine is a beautiful place. You step through the front door into a dark hallway filled with the cool, earthy smell of stored apples, quince, and gourds somewhere nearby. As your eyes adjust, you'll notice brightly painted walls and a winding staircase laid with terracotta tiles. The echoey stairs lead to a dining room dressed with a wooden table, a few chairs, and an open fireplace in the corner. A door off the dining room leads to their famous walk-in pantry, which served as my great-aunt Régine's kitchen when she was alive.

There has always been a jam of people in this house. In World War II, my great-grandfather, Aimé, hid Vichy defectors here for two years along with a cache of weapons parachuted in by the British to aid the Resistance network, of which he was a part. Later, Papé Aimé bequeathed La Touraine to his daughter Régine, and she and her husband, Jo, planted their lush *potager* and hosted unforgettable meals here for all of us.

Serves 4

pinch of salt

2 teaspoons red wine vinegar

2 tablespoons olive oil

4 endives (approx. 14 oz/400 g)

2 eating apples, such as Fuji or Golden Delicious, peeled, cored, and sliced into 1¼ inch (3 cm) chunks

5½ oz (150 g) Roquefort, cut into ½ inch (1 cm) pieces

½ cup (1¾ oz/50 g) walnut halves, left whole or chopped

5½ oz (150 g) black olives (un-pitted, à la Grecque), drained

freshly ground black pepper

Prepare the dressing in a large salad bowl: dissolve the salt in the vinegar, then add some ground black pepper, followed by the olive oil. Whisk with a fork.

Trim the base of the endives, then slice widthways into 1 inch (2 cm) rounds: these should fall apart into segments which can then be added to the salad bowl. Follow with the apples, Roquefort, walnuts, and olives. Toss the salad gently to coat all the ingredients in the dressing, then serve immediately. The olive pits are left on the side of the plates after eating.

celeriac, carrot, and red onion salad

Dress this crunchy salad according to your fancy or the dishes it is accompanying: a few tablespoons of plain yogurt and a whole-grain mustard for something resembling a remoulade; to keep it fresh, simply use olive oil, salt, and lemon juice to taste. Or, to make it into more of a coleslaw, stir in a few tablespoons of homemade Mayonnaise (see page 198). All three versions would make a fine accompaniment to roast chicken.

Serves 6

3 carrots, peeled

½ celeriac (celery root; approx. 1 lb 2 oz/ 500 g), peeled

1 large red (or sweet white) onion, finely sliced

Use a cheese grater (or an electric food processor with a grating attachment) to coarsely grate the carrots and celeriac. Add the carrots, celeriac, and onion to a large salad bowl, then stir in the mixed dressing of your choosing. Serve immediately; any leftovers will be good for a day.

THREE DRESSING OPTIONS

Fresh
6–8 tablespoons olive oil; juice of ½ lemon; 1 garlic clove, crushed; 2 handfuls of chopped herbs, such as parsley, mint, and cilantro; and salt and freshly ground black pepper, to taste.

Remoulade
1¼ cups (300 ml) Greek or plain yogurt; 1 tablespoon whole-grain mustard; 3 tablespoons olive oil; and salt and freshly ground black pepper, to taste.

Coleslaw
1¼ cups (300 ml) Mayonnaise (see page 198); and salt and freshly ground black pepper, to taste.

salade frisée

curly endive salad

Serves 2–6

For 2 people

6½ oz (180 g) frisée

big pinch of salt

2½ teaspoons red wine vinegar

½ garlic clove, crushed

big pinch of freshly ground
black pepper

3 tablespoons olive oil

For 5–6 people

1 lb (450 g) frisée

¼ teaspoon salt

1 tablespoon red wine vinegar

2 garlic cloves, crushed

¼ teaspoon freshly ground
black pepper

5–6 tablespoons olive oil

Optional extras

Smoked lardons: 1¾ oz (50 g)
per person, fried until crispy

Eggs: 1 per person, poached

Gizzards: 2½ oz (70 g) per
person, pan-fried in oil until
cooked through

Croutons (see page 199):
1 handful per person

Frisée is the truly classic French salad, almost always served with
a garlic dressing. For this reason, it is perfect with steak, or pies
and gratins such as the Seafood Vol-au-Vents (see page 183) or
Brandade Parmentière (see page 49), since the sharp vinaigrette-
coated leaves cut through these dishes' inherent richness.

Below are basic guidelines for dressing ever-increasing
quantities of frisée. Whisk the dressing in the base of the salad
bowl, taste it, then make little adjustments according to likes
and preferences. My great-uncle Roland, for example, never
puts more than a soupçon of vinegar in his dressings, preferring
the olive oil to take the lead.

There is a pared-back elegance to starting a dinner party
with a salade frisée and fresh baguette. At big gatherings, the
sight of my mother tossing a vast quantity of this salad for all
of us is a familiar one. However, to make a frisée salad into a
main course, toss in some fried smoked lardons or gizzards and
provide a poached egg per person, known as a salade Lyonnaise.
In summer, I often add a few sliced, ripe tomatoes.

Pull as many leaves as are needed off the head of frisée. Check
the leaves and tear off and discard any parts that have gone soft
and dark. Soak the leaves in a sink filled with fresh water for a few
minutes. If there is a lot of sediment at the bottom, change the
water and wash the leaves a second time, otherwise thoroughly dry
the salad in batches in a salad spinner. Set aside.

Prepare the dressing: In a large salad bowl, dissolve the salt in the
vinegar. Add the garlic, followed by the black pepper and olive oil.
Lightly whisk with a fork and taste to check the seasoning, making
any adjustments as necessary. Place the washed and dried leaves on
top of the dressing, tearing any very big leaves in half. Toss, then
eat immediately.

one soup, two courses

There's nothing like coming home and having dinner waiting for you. When my great-grandparents and their ancestors would head out to work in our fields, they would return to the house at midday for a bit of lunch and to put *la soupe* on for supper. Vegetables and some salt pork, if available, were chopped and placed in a big pot filled with fresh water. Left covered, in the corner of the fire in the early 1900s and then on a wood-fired stove a few decades later, the pot would sit and gently simmer until sunset and, when they arrived back home, from one pot, a two-course meal was ready.

Similar to pot-au-feu or poule-au-pot, from one load of simmered vegetables you get two courses: a first from the cooking broth, ladled over bread that has been toasted, rubbed with garlic, and drizzled with olive oil. Grated Emmental can also be added liberally, if not extravagantly, in the case of greedy children. For the second course, the vegetables are strained from any remaining broth in the pan and served. Each diner then adds their own dressing to their plate of steaming vegetables: a crushed garlic clove, lots of olive oil, salt, black pepper, vinegar…

There are lots of names for this dish in Provence, La Baïana being my favorite iteration. Ingredients and cooking times vary according to the season and the grandmother cooking it, longer in winter for simmering root crops, and shorter in springtime when vegetables are tender and sweet. What follows is the recipe as described to me by my great-aunt Edmée through the branches of a cherry tree as we harvested together one morning. I have made adjustments to the lengthy fireside cooking time Edmée described to me, since modern tastes, kitchens, and requirements call for this.

Serves 4

For the soup

1 cup (7 oz/200 g) brown lentils

1½ tablespoons (¾ oz/20 g) butter

7 oz (200 g) smoked lardons

1 potato, peeled and diced into ½ inch (1 cm) chunks

3 carrots, peeled and diced into ½ inch (1 cm) chunks

1 large leek, sliced into ½ inch (1 cm) rounds

2 celery sticks, diced into ½ inch (1 cm) chunks

4 slices of crusty bread

1 garlic clove, halved

To serve (on the table)

grated cheese (Emmental or Cheddar)

olive oil

red wine vinegar

garlic and garlic press

salt and freshly ground black pepper

SOUPE DE LENTILLES AU PETIT SALÉ

two-course lentil and lardon soup

Tolerance levels to wet bread varies from person to person. For this soup, I like my bread to reach a crouton level of crispness and, as such, take care to use already stale bread, brushing it with olive oil and toasting it in the oven for 10 minutes.

Check the lentils over for any grit, then rinse in a sieve and set aside.

Melt the butter in a Dutch oven or heavy-bottomed pot. Add the lardons and fry over medium heat until colored but not crispy. Add the prepared vegetables and lentils to the pot and cover with 8½ cups (2 liters) of cold water. Simmer, covered, for 1¼ hours.

When the soup is almost ready, prepare the bread by toasting the slices, then rubbing them with the cut side of the garlic clove. Call everyone to the table, and place the pot of soup in the middle. Once everyone is seated, place a slice of bread in each soup bowl and encourage diners to sprinkle on cheese, black pepper, and olive oil over liberally. Ladle the cooking broth over the prepared bread. Eat immediately.

Once ready for the second course, use a slotted spoon to dish out the cooked lentils, lardons, and vegetables. Each diner will drizzle over their own olive oil and vinegar and add crushed garlic, salt, and black pepper to taste.

poichichade

"Any half-decent poichichade has thirteen ingredients," I was told by a seller in Carpentras market once. Akin to hummus, poichichade is a Provençal chickpea purée, served cold for *apéro* with toasted bread and crudités, or hot as an alternative to mashed potatoes with roasted meat. I left the gentleman's stall none the wiser about these thirteen mysterious ingredients, but laden with three tubs of his poichichade and a determination to try and identify at least half of them. His recipe will remain his Provençal family secret, as it should, but in his honor, here is my own recipe for thirteen-ingredient poichichade.

Serves 6

1 lb 2 oz (500 g) dried chickpeas, (or 4 x 14 oz/ 400 g cans of chickpeas)

5 tablespoons olive oil

2 carrots, peeled and diced

1 large onion, diced

1 celery stick, diced

2 garlic cloves, crushed

2 bay leaves

2 teaspoons ground cumin

2 teaspoons ground coriander

1 teaspoon cayenne pepper

2 cups (500 ml) chicken or vegetable stock

juice of 1 lemon

salt and freshly ground black pepper

If using dried chickpeas, soak overnight in cold water, then fast-simmer in fresh unsalted water until tender, about 40 minutes.

Heat the olive oil in a heavy-bottomed pot over medium–low heat and add the carrots, onion, and celery. Sweat for 20 minutes, putting the lid on from time to time to encourage the vegetables to steam a little in their own juices. Then add the garlic, followed by the bay leaves, cumin, coriander, cayenne pepper, and black pepper. Cook for a further 1 minute, then turn off the heat and remove the bay leaves.

Prepare the stock. Drain the cooked or canned chickpeas and add them to the pot, along with a big splash of the stock. Using a handheld immersion blender, purée the chickpeas and vegetables, adding the remaining stock incrementally, until you achieve a very creamy mash consistency. Add lemon juice and salt to taste.

If you are serving the poichichade as a dip with crudités, decant it into a bowl, and finish with an extra 2 tablespoons of olive oil and more black pepper on top.

If you are eating the poichichade hot alongside a meat course, keep it in the pot. Five minutes before you would like to serve it, add a splash or two of additional water or stock and place the pot over medium heat. Quickly bring to a simmer, stirring continuously, then serve.

baguette pizzas

Using baguette as a base, we often make delicious "pizzas" using anything lurking in the fridge. I enjoy making each baguette pizza look different.

Serves 2–3

For the bases

1 day-old baguette (about 22 in/56 cm long)

½ quantity of Sauce Tomate (see page 74), or 2 cups (500 ml) tomato coulis (see page 76) or ready-made tomato sauce

olive oil (optional)

1 onion, chopped (optional)

14 oz (400 g) can chopped tomatoes (optional)

salt and freshly ground black pepper (optional)

For the toppings

1 ball of mozzarella, sliced

3 tablespoons grated cheese

1 teaspoon capers

4 anchovy fillets

1 oz (30 g) cooked or cured ham or chorizo, sliced or chopped

For the garnish

2 big pinches of dried thyme

1 tablespoon olive oil

freshly ground black pepper

Preheat the oven to 400°F (200°C). For the bases, cut the baguette into two or three pieces, then slice each piece lengthways. Place, cut-side up, on a baking pan.

If you don't have any leftover sauce tomate, tomato coulis, or ready-made sauce available, fry the chopped onion in a little olive oil for 15 minutes, then stir in the can of tomatoes and plenty of salt and black pepper.

Spoon the sauce over the baguettes, then add the toppings. Finish with the thyme, olive oil, and black pepper. Bake in the oven for 12 minutes, and enjoy immediately.

gratin de morue

salt cod gratin

Not so long ago, the fountains of Provençal villages would fill with soaking salt cod on Friday mornings. Friday was, of course, a day of abstinence from red meat and for people living inland, morue was the alternative.

My grandfather's partner, Violette, remembers the squabbles at the fountain in our village when people came to collect their desalted fish and inevitably forgot whose was whose. No one was likely to mistake my great-aunt's mother-in-law Louise Boudin's morue for theirs, since she'd soak it in her toilet cistern. Her reason being that it was as close as she could get to a running stream of water, like the village fountains. Every time someone pulled the chain, the old soaking water would drain from the cistern and it would refill with fresh drinking water. While Louise's logic is sound, readers should perhaps consider a more conventional soaking method. Additionally, check the salt cod package instructions or ask the fishmonger how long the fillets require soaking: 24 hours is average but it can be as little as four or as many as 48 hours.

This delicious gratin is humble in appearance but quite luxurious in reality. It's an assembly job of creamed spinach, poached salt cod, parboiled potatoes, tomatoes, and delicious olive oil. Theoretically, one could prepare it in advance and keep in the fridge before cooking in the oven for just a little longer than is indicated opposite.

Serves 4–6

1 lb 5 oz (600 g) salt cod

1 bay leaf

1 lb 2 oz (500 g) fresh spinach

generous ¾ cup (200 ml) olive oil

1 large onion, finely chopped

1 cup (2 oz/60 g) fresh breadcrumbs

1 garlic clove, crushed

generous ¾ cup (200 ml) milk

1 cup (9 oz/250 g) crème fraîche

14 oz (400 g) potatoes

⅔ cup (3½ oz/100 g) cherry tomatoes, quartered

salt and freshly ground black pepper

A day before you wish to serve the gratin, rinse off any excess salt from the cod and place in the fridge in a large bowl of water for 24 hours, changing the water every 3–4 hours, where possible.

The following day, preheat the oven to 400°F (200°C). Fill a saucepan with fresh water, add the bay leaf, then bring to a boil. Lower the heat, add the fish, and poach for 8–10 minutes, then drain and place on a board. Using a fork, separate the flesh into flakes, checking thoroughly for any bones and removing them with tweezers. Place in a bowl and set aside.

Wash the spinach, then place the leaves directly in a large saucepan over medium–high heat: no cooking water is necessary since the droplets clinging to the leaves after their rinse will suffice for the task. Wilt the leaves, using tongs to continuously turn them in the saucepan and cook evenly. Once all the leaves have wilted, drain in a colander, then place on a board and roughly chop.

Next, place a few tablespoons of the olive oil in a large frying pan over low heat. Add the chopped onion and gently sweat for about 15 minutes, until soft and translucent. Add all but 2 tablespoons of the breadcrumbs, the garlic, and a few extra tablespoons of the olive oil. Stir and cook for 1 minute to take the bite from the garlic, then stir in the chopped spinach, milk, and crème fraîche. Gently cook, stirring, for a few minutes, just until everything is well incorporated and the spinach takes on a creamy consistency. Add black pepper and a modest sprinkling of salt.

Peel the potatoes and slice into ⅛ inch (5 mm) thick rounds, placing in the rinsed saucepan you used to poach your fish or your spinach as you go. Cover with fresh water, then bring to a boil and fast-simmer for 8 minutes. Drain and set aside.

Assemble your gratin: drizzle some olive oil in the base of a medium-sized, preferably earthenware, pie dish. Spoon a layer of creamed spinach at the bottom and follow with a loose layer of potatoes, a few tablespoons of salt cod flakes, and two or three cherry tomatoes. Drizzle over some olive oil and repeat the sequence. Continue layering, not forgetting the olive oil, until you have used up all the ingredients, aiming to finish with a layer of spinach. Sprinkle over the remaining breadcrumbs, then bake for 25 minutes. Serve with delicious white or rosé wine.

bourride

Bourride involves a few steps but is so very worth the trouble: white fish and shrimp are briefly poached in a broth, then lifted out and placed in soup bowls. A freshly prepared aïoli is then whisked into the poaching liquid, thickening it and rendering it an exquisite color. This sauce is then poured over the waiting seafood in bowls. A firm variety of fish that will hold its shape when poaching is preferable, but other than this, bourride can be made with any seafood available. Perhaps a lovely piece of haddock and some cooked shrimp from the supermarket. Or, for a special occasion, a filleted monkfish and some squid from the fishmonger.

Serves 2

For the aïoli

1 garlic clove, peeled

1 egg yolk

scant ½ cup (100 ml) olive oil

pinch of salt

squeeze of lemon juice

For the soup

2 tablespoons (1 oz/30 g) butter

2 shallots, finely sliced

1 leek, sliced into ½ inch (1 cm) rounds

1 clove

1⅔ cups (400 ml) fish stock (fresh or from a bouillon cube)

pinch of saffron threads

pinch of piment d'espelette or cayenne pepper

2 potatoes, peeled and diced

squeeze of lemon juice

14 oz (400 g) firm white fish fillet, such as monkfish, haddock, or cod loin

3½ oz (100 g) raw, large peeled shrimp (or a squid, prepared and sliced)

freshly ground black pepper

toasted bread, to serve

First prepare the aïoli: crush the garlic clove into a bowl and add the egg yolk. Whisk together, then add a few drops of the olive oil. Whisk again, then add more of the olive oil. Continue in this way, adding the oil very gradually and whisking until you have used it all and created your aïoli: it should look like a few tablespoons of very yellow mayonnaise. Finish with the pinch of salt and a few drops of lemon juice to taste. Set aside in the fridge.

Next, begin the soup. Place the butter in a saucepan over low heat and, once melted, add the shallots and leek. Soften, with the lid on, for 10–15 minutes, stirring frequently.

Meanwhile, grind the clove using a mortar and pestle. Prepare the stock: reheating it if fresh, or dissolving a fish bouillon cube in boiling water, if not. In a small bowl, steep the saffron threads in a few tablespoons of boiling water.

Add the ground clove to the cooked shallots and leek, along with the pinch of piment d'espelette, the saffron liquid, and some black pepper. Pour in the fish stock and stir. Add the potatoes, then bring the broth to a simmer.

Divide the fish fillet into two equal pieces if not already, then lower into the liquid. Poach for 8–10 minutes, turning over halfway if the broth doesn't cover the fish completely, then add the shrimp. A few minutes later, once the shrimp are pink and the fillet opaque, turn off the heat. Check the fish is cooked by teasing it with a knife and ensuring the flakes separate easily. Squeeze over some lemon juice.

Using a slotted spoon, lift the fish, vegetables, and shrimp out of the liquid and distribute between two soup bowls. Add just over half of the prepared aïoli to the liquid remaining in the pan and whisk. Heat through over low heat, then pour the sauce over the waiting bowls of fish. Serve immediately with toasted bread spread with the remaining aïoli.

leg of lamb with tapenade

Slow-cooked leg of lamb has become popular in recent years and, while delicious, in Provence it is more common to fast-roast legs in a hot oven and serve them pink. Rosemary and bashed garlic are the classic aromatics, but for something different, leftover tapenade and anchovies lend a wonderful depth to the meat. Serve carved pieces of this lamb on hot Poichichade (see page 161) for an elegant main course.

Serves 8

4½ lb (2 kg) bone-in leg of lamb

6 anchovies

2–3 tablespoons black olive Tapenade (see page 120)

4 tablespoons olive oil

sprinkling of sea salt flakes

2 teaspoons freshly ground black pepper

Remove the leg of lamb from the fridge at least 1 hour before cooking. Preheat the oven to 475°F (240°C) and place the meat in a medium-sized roasting pan so it fits snugly.

Finely chop the anchovies and stir into the tapenade. Smear the mixture all over the meat and drizzle with the olive oil. Add the sprinkling of salt flakes and the black pepper, then place in the oven.

After 15 minutes, lower the temperature to 425°F (220°C). Roast the leg for a total of 15–18 minutes per 1 lb (450 g) to serve beautifully pink in the center, or for a little longer if you prefer it well done. Turn the leg once, halfway through cooking. Once the meat has finished roasting, rest on the counter, covered in foil, for 10 minutes before carving and serving.

lapin de violette

For this dish, rabbit is marinated and browned, then gently simmered for a few hours. The result is not a stew, but rather a herby, aromatic meat, falling off the bone, very nice served with a little of its cooking jus on a bed of long-grain or Camargue rice, or some warmed butter beans. The 3½ lb (1.6 kg) of meat I suggest here is usually equivalent to two rabbits. Ask what the butcher can provide (wild rabbits are smaller) and consider that a 7 oz (200 g) variance in either direction will not make much difference.

Serves 6

3½ lb (1.6 kg) rabbit(s)

about 6 tablespoons olive oil

1 teaspoon freshly ground
black pepper

6 shallots, halved

4 garlic cloves, lightly bashed
in their skins

2 teaspoons dried thyme

4 sprigs of rosemary

5 bay leaves

juice of 1 lemon

2 cups (500 ml) white wine

2 celery sticks, roughly diced

1 tablespoon all-purpose flour

3½ oz (100 g) green olives

1½ cups (350 ml) boiling water

salt

Place a rabbit on a chopping board and cut into joints with a sharp knife: Slice off and separate the shoulders and legs. Chop the saddle into four pieces (or two if it is a little rabbit). Remove and discard the head, kidneys, and liver if desired. Repeat the process for the second rabbit.

Place the meat in a large, non-metallic bowl and drizzle with 3 tablespoons of the olive oil and some black pepper. Add the shallots, garlic cloves, thyme, rosemary, bay leaves, lemon juice, and wine. Cover and marinate for at least 2 hours (or overnight) in the fridge, stirring the meat once or twice to ensure all sides get a turn in the liquid.

Once the meat has finished marinating, drizzle 2 tablespoons of the remaining olive oil in a large Dutch oven or heavy-bottomed pot over medium heat. Using tongs, remove the rabbit pieces from the marinade and brown the meat in batches, setting the cooked pieces aside in another bowl as you go. This will take about 15 minutes and you will need to add a little extra olive oil in between batches.

Once you have finished browning the meat, lower the heat. Add the celery to the pot. Using a slotted spoon, lift out the herbs, garlic, and shallots from the marinade bowl (reserving the marinade liquid for later) and transfer to the pot. Add a little more olive oil if needed.

Gently cook the herby vegetables, stirring to ensure they don't catch, for about 15 minutes, then add the flour. Continue to cook for a few minutes, stirring constantly. At this stage, raise the heat and return the rabbit to the pot, along with the reserved marinade liquid.

Allow to bubble for 5 minutes, then lower the heat to a gentle simmer and add the boiling water and some salt. Push all the meat under the simmering sauce as much as possible (the pieces should be packed like sardines), then cover the pot and simmer for at least 2 hours, stirring from time to time.

The dish is ready once the meat slides off the bones. About 15 minutes before you are ready to serve, remove the lid and stir in the olives. Serve hot with mashed potatoes or rice.

civet de sanglier

wild boar civet

For a time, my great-grandfather Aimé bred wild boar. I have heard stories about a particularly taciturn stud named Gaspard for whom everyone seems to have had a soft spot despite his grumpy outlook. Wild boar civet takes time and patience, but the result is a beautiful ragout that can be served on mashed potatoes, or with pappardelle (if serving as a pasta dish, the quantity here goes much further). A glass of the animal's blood was traditionally added at the end to thicken the sauce, but since this is an uncommon practice in modern cooking, the contents of a blood sausage called "boudin noir" is sometimes crumbled in instead. Although this recipe includes flour to account for the absence of blood or suitable blood sausage, if the sauce is still quite runny before serving, remove the meat and vegetables from the pan using a slotted spoon, turn up the heat, and reduce the liquid to the desired consistency before returning the meat to the pan and serving.

Serves 8

4½ lb (2 kg) diced wild boar

2 x 750 ml bottles of full-bodied red wine

⅔ cup (150 ml) red wine vinegar

4 bay leaves

6 dried juniper berries

1 tablespoon dried thyme

3½ oz (100 g) unsmoked lardons

1 teaspoon freshly ground black pepper

6 garlic cloves, finely sliced

3 onions, cut into eighths

generous ¾ cup (3½ oz/100 g) all-purpose flour

generous ¾ cup (200 ml) olive oil

2 heaped tablespoons tomato paste

5½ oz (150 g) black olives

3 oz (80 g) boudin noir (optional)

mashed potatoes or tagliatelle, to serve

Place the boar meat in a large, non-metallic bowl. Add the wine, vinegar, bay leaves, juniper berries, thyme, lardons, black pepper, garlic, and onions. Mix, cover, and leave to marinate in the fridge for 2 days.

After the boar has finished marinating, separate the meat, onions, and aromatics from the marinade by pouring everything into a colander set over a bowl. Place the flour on a plate. Pat-dry the boar pieces with paper towels, then roll in the plate of flour to coat.

Place an extra-large, heavy-bottomed pot over medium heat. Add 3 tablespoons of the olive oil, then brown the chunks of boar in batches, adding extra oil with each batch. Remove from the pot and set aside. Add the aromatics, lardons, and onions to the emptied pot and cook for 15 minutes, stirring very frequently. Once the onions have become soft, place the browned meat back in the pot and pour over the reserved marinade. Bring to a fast simmer, then stir in the tomato paste. Cover and simmer over the lowest heat for 4–6 hours, until the meat is completely tender.

About 45 minutes before serving, drain the olives and add them to the pot. Keep the lid off and turn the heat up slightly. Remove the skin from the boudin noir, if using, and crumble in. Continue to simmer, uncovered, while you prepare any accompaniments.

Stir a final few tablespoons of olive oil into the pot just before serving. This dish gets better with time so could also happily be served the day after cooking.

pâté

Tata Edmée remembers the pig being slaughtered every year at La Cointe during the spring. Making the most of every last morsel involved great and swift work for the family, but it meant that, for a time, they ate like kings. Prime cuts were roasted, salt-cured, dried, and boiled. Offcuts were transformed into sausages, saucissons, pâtés, boudins, and terrines. The cured ham, saucissons and, particularly, the salted pork belly, or "lardons" in their modern guise, were eked out over the year. This year-round availability of salt-cured pork is why lardons are such a staple ingredient in a great number of classic French country soup and stew recipes, ever popular today.

Here and now, for those of us short of a home-reared pig, chicken liver pâtés are delicious, hearty, and very easy to make. This recipe is French, rather than Provençal specifically, but it has become a part of our Christmas Day menu in lieu of foie gras, with a glass of Sauternes and some pain brioché.

Serves 8

2¼ sticks (9 oz/250 g) softened butter

3–4 shallots, finely chopped

3 dried juniper berries

14 oz (400 g) chicken livers, gristle discarded

scant ½ cup (100 ml) cognac

salt and freshly ground black pepper

Melt 1½ tablespoons (¾ oz/20 g) of the butter in a frying pan over low heat. Add the shallots and soften for 10 minutes. While the shallots are cooking, crush the juniper berries using a mortar and pestle. Once the shallots have softened, turn the heat up and add the chicken livers, plenty of black pepper, and the crushed juniper berries. Sauté for 10 minutes, stirring frequently and adding additional butter if required, until the chicken livers are cooked to your liking.

Spoon the cooked livers and shallots into a food processor. Place the empty frying pan back over medium heat, add the cognac, and deglaze. Bubble the alcohol away until it has reduced by half, then pour into the food processor over the livers and shallots. Add all but 4 tablespoons (2 oz/60 g) of the remaining butter, and a pinch of salt, then blend until a smooth consistency has been obtained.

Decant the pâté into a terrine dish. Level the surface. Melt the remaining 4 tablespoons (2 oz/60 g) of butter in a small saucepan over medium heat, then pour over the top of your pâté to create an airtight seal. Place the pâté in the fridge to set for at least 3 hours.

Serve scoops or slices of pâté alongside warm toasted bread, and a lamb lettuce salad, lightly dressed with a sweet vinaigrette.

daube

Daube is the truly classic Provençal winter stew. Somber in aspect yet celebratory enough to redeem the worst day of vine-pruning, battered by a freezing mistral. Prepare the daube the day before you wish to eat it and reheat slowly, for at least 1½ hours before serving. A lidded, cast-iron pot is best. Consider that, wine and meat aside, the most important ingredients are the orange peel and anchovies: do not be put off by their apparent discordancy, they have important jobs to do. I serve daube with creamy mashed potatoes, though it is commonly accompanied by tagliatelle in Provence, like ragù.

Serves 8

generous ¾ cup (3½ oz/100 g) all-purpose flour

4½ lb (2 kg) ox cheeks (about 4), fat trimmed

6–8 tablespoons sunflower oil

2 large carrots, peeled and roughly chopped

2 celery sticks, roughly chopped

14 oz (400 g) shallots, halved

2 sprigs of rosemary

1 teaspoon dried thyme

3 bay leaves

4 garlic cloves, finely sliced

1¾ oz (50 g) anchovy fillets

750 ml bottle of red wine

14 oz (400 g) can of chopped tomatoes

peel of 1 orange

2–3 tablespoons olive oil

salt and freshly ground black pepper

Place the flour in a bowl. Halve the ox cheeks and roll them in the flour to coat.

Place an extra-large Dutch oven or ovenproof pot for which you have a lid over medium heat. Add 2 tablespoons of the sunflower oil to begin, then brown the meat in batches, drizzling in more oil if the pot ever looks dry with each subsequent batch. Set aside the seared meat in another bowl as you go.

Once you have finished browning the cheeks, lower the heat and pour in a little more sunflower oil. Add the chopped vegetables, along with the rosemary, thyme, and bay leaves. Stir for a few minutes, then cover the pot to gently sweat.

Preheat the oven to 325°F (160°C).

Keep an eye on the cooking vegetables, lifting the lid and stirring every so often. After the carrots, celery, and shallots have softened for 20 minutes, add the garlic and anchovies. Stir until the anchovies have dissolved, then return the meat to the pot.

Turn the heat up to high and pour in the wine. Bring to a fast simmer for a few minutes, then add the tomatoes. Follow with the orange peel and some salt and black pepper. Stir, then press all of the meat into the liquid so it is as immersed as possible. Cover and gently cook in the oven for 4 hours.

After 4 hours, check the meat is tender: the cheeks should easily come apart when teased. Stir in the olive oil, then serve immediately. Alternatively, cool overnight, then reheat slowly for 1½ hours before serving the following day.

vin d'orange

When I went to our cooperative cave Terraventoux in January once and asked for 10 liters of white wine *en vrac** the keeper Vincent gave me a look and said: "*Vin d'orange?*" Either Vincent could read minds or I wasn't the only person after vast quantities of *vrac* that day. Vin d'orange is a refreshing and subtly-spiced apéritif, served chilled. Like Italy's limoncello, it is one of those drinks that families in Provence make themselves.

To make, sliced oranges, spices, sugar, fruit eau de vie, and wine are macerated together for a few months. That's it. Commercially, the most alcoholic eau de vie you can buy is 45 proof and it is usually flavored with the fruit from whence it was double-distilled. This flavor, of course, affects the final drink, so use as neutral a fruit eau de vie as you can find, and if you have access to some legitimate 180 proof (90%) alcohol from, say, Italy or some US states, where it is legal, add 1⅔ cups (400 ml) here instead of the 4¼ cups (1 liter) of 90 proof (45%) spirit suggested.

You will need a 2–2½ gallon (8–10 liter) wide-mouth demijohn or glass drinks dispenser. One could, of course, make a smaller quantity, proportionately reducing the amounts indicated below, but I will say that vin d'orange is absolutely worth making in bulk, since you are only likely to make this once a year and a bottle is a really special thing to bring to people as a gift.

Makes 8 bottles

5¼ quarts (5 liters) dry white or rosé wine (6⅔ x 750 ml bottles)

3¾ cups (1 lb 10½ oz/750 g) sugar

4¼ cups (1 liter) 90 proof (45%) fruit eau de vie

7 oranges, washed and quartered

1 Seville (bitter) orange, washed and quartered

1 cinnamon stick

2 cloves

Pour the wine, sugar, and eau de vie into a demijohn or glass drinks dispenser. Stirring with a long implement, dissolve the sugar in the liquid. Add all the orange quarters to the demijohn, along with the cinnamon stick and cloves. Place the lid on and leave to macerate for 2 months out of direct sunlight, giving it a swill every so often.

After 2 months, the aromatics can be discarded and the vin d'orange bottled. Ready about eight wine bottles and corks, ensuring they are thoroughly cleaned and dried before use.

If the drink has been macerating in a demijohn, remove the lid and carefully pour as much vin d'orange as will fit in a large, clean jug. Remove the quartered oranges and spices, then wait for any smaller floating particles to sink to the bottom. If the drink has been macerating in a glass drinks dispenser, simply open the tap to fill the jug. Decant the drink into bottles, leaving behind any orange bits from the bottom of the jug. Cork and label the bottles.

*Straight from the barrel, one euro a liter, BYO bottle.

croquants aux amandes

almond bites

My parents built their house on an old almond orchard and there are still plenty of sweet and bitter varieties growing in their garden. We always forget which tree is which, resulting in plenty of spat out almonds over the years. Aside from the fact that they taste awful, raw bitter almonds yield cyanide when ingested. However, used in small amounts or as an extract, bitter almonds are a common pâtisserie ingredient, responsible for that telltale aroma synonymous with marzipan. Old Italian recipes, such as Patience Gray's for amaretti in *Honey from a Weed,* suggest traditional uses for whole bitter almonds, if of interest.

What follows is my great-aunt Tata Edmée's recipe for classic almond croquants. At Christmas, she often produces a tin of these crumbly, crunchy cookies for the *goûter* to serve alongside coffee or a tisane.

Makes 30

generous ½ cup (3 oz/80 g) shelled whole almonds

generous ¾ cup (3½ oz/100 g) all-purpose flour

¾ cup (5½ oz/150 g) sugar

1 egg

pinch of salt

2 drops of bitter almond extract (or 1 bitter almond)

Preheat the oven to 400°F (200°C) and line a baking sheet with parchment paper.

Begin by toasting the almonds: place them in a dry frying pan over medium heat. Toast for 1–2 minutes, standing by and shaking the pan to avoid any burning (which can happen very quickly). Cool on a board, then roughly chop with a sharp knife.

In a large bowl, mix the flour, sugar, and egg together. The texture should be quite crumbly, yet hold together when pressed, like a rough marzipan. Add the chopped almonds, using your hands to distribute the pieces evenly throughout the mixture. Divide the mixture in half and place in two piles on the prepared baking sheet. Use your fingers to press the piles into two rectangular shapes, each approximately ½ inch (1 cm) thick.

Place in the oven and bake for 25–30 minutes until lightly golden, crisp-looking, and offering some resistance when pressed. Allow to cool slightly, then slice widthways into finger-sized segments. Oven temperatures vary and if the insides still look a little soft after slicing, do not panic, the croquants will still be delicious, just chewy rather than crunchy. Once cool, store in an airtight container.

chocolate orange gâteau

For this dessert, walnuts are paired with their winter fruit bowl companions and the result is an intense, exceedingly moist dessert, which will keep for days: a rustic spin on the classic flourless orange and almond Passover cake, and an excellent dinner-party dessert with a dollop of creamy mascarpone on the side.

Serves 10

2 oranges

2 cups (7 oz/200 g) walnuts (plus a handful extra for decoration, if you wish)

6 eggs

1¼ cups (9 oz/250 g) sugar

2 teaspoons baking powder

2 tablespoons unsweetened cocoa powder

1 cup (9 oz/250 g) mascarpone, to serve

Place the oranges in a saucepan, cover with plenty of water, put a lid on, and bring to a boil. Lower the heat slightly and fast-simmer for 1 hour, then drain and allow the oranges to cool completely in a colander.

Once cool enough to handle, tear the oranges into pieces in the colander, allowing any excess liquid to drain away. Carefully remove any seeds or stalk stubs. Then, using a handheld immersion blender or food processor, purée the oranges, peel, pith, and all, to a pulp and set aside (or place in the fridge if you are baking the cake the following day).

Preheat the oven to 400°F (200°C) and grease and line a 10 inch (25 cm) round cake pan with parchment paper. Blend the walnuts to as fine a "flour" as you can in a food processor (though a few bigger crumbs aren't anything to worry about). Transfer to a mixing bowl, along with the puréed oranges.

Crack the eggs into a separate large mixing bowl and whisk for a minute. Add the sugar and continue to whisk for a minute or two. Add the baking and cocoa powders, whisk again, then finally, add the walnuts and blended oranges and gently stir to homogenize.

Pour the mixture into your prepared cake pan and bake in the middle of the oven for 45 minutes to 1 hour. Test the cake is cooked after 45 minutes by skewering the center with a toothpick and checking it comes out clean. If the cake needs more time but the top is browning more than you would like, cover with foil and put it back in the oven.

Remove from the oven once cooked. After a minute or two, remove from the pan and cool on a wire rack: to do this, run a knife around the side of the pan, then carefully tip it upside down onto a large plate, then invert onto the wire rack. Top with walnut halves, for decoration. Slice and serve with a dollop of mascarpone on the side.

CHRISTMAS

Christmas in Provence is very special. Bakeries and chocolate shops fill with whole candied fruit and *papillotes*. Even the smallest, most isolated hamlet will display beautiful twinkling lights and decorations in the streets. In homes, along with Christmas trees, *santons de Provence*, little terracotta figurines, are arranged in the nativity scene on moss collected from the woods: *La Crèche*. On Christmas Eve, slippers, *les pantoufles*, are left under the tree, so *Papa Noël* will know who to leave presents for, and come midnight, we toast with the homemade liqueurs like Vin d'Orange (see page 174) or vin de noix, prepared months before. Breakfast on Christmas morning is generally a sweet fougasse or a Pompe à Huile (see page 191) around the fire with some coffee or hot chocolate, but we try not to eat too much, since the lunchtime meal is lavish and starts early, at twelve thirty pm promptly.

You will not find recipes for our complete family Christmas Day menu here since, in reality, many elements are purchased ready-to-eat: smoked salmon, oysters (though, of course, these need to be shucked), the sorbet and booze for the *trou norman*, the cheeses… Where appropriate, I have provided recipes, for example, for the truffled brie served with the cheese course, or the wonderful cardoon in white sauce. However, we are not one of those frightfully elegant families that serves duck or goose on Christmas day I'm afraid, and I decided that the world doesn't need another turkey and stuffing recipe, so this will be up to you to seek elsewhere. What may come as a shock is that we eat the turkey, gravy, and stuffing without any trimmings after the cardoon course (pretty much the only vegetable in sight at this meal). Perhaps, you will understand why it has to be this way when you see what is coming for dessert: a banquet table dedicated to Les Treize Desserts (see page 190), the thirteen desserts.

I imagine some of you will take comfort in the fact that you don't have to make all of this for Christmas Day. Rest assured that we share the load, too, as an extended family. So, regardless of whether you (and a small army of helpers) are going to give the full Provençal Christmas menu a try, or whether you're going to just make the orangettes from the treize desserts… *Joyeux Noël!*

christmas eve menu

Apéritif
Marquisette *(see page 181)*

Main Course
Seafood Vol-au-Vents *(see page 183)*
Frisée

---

christmas day menu

Apéritif
Brandade Truffée *(see page 186)*
Toasted Baguette
(Champagne)

First Course
Oysters
Smoked Salmon
Baguette, Butter, and Lemon Wedges
(Viognier)

Second Course
Chicken Liver Pâté *(see page 172)*
Plum Chutney *(see page 112)*
Lamb lettuce
Brioche Bread
(Sauterne)

Palate cleanser
Le Trou Norman à la Poire: A Shot of Poire
Williams on a Scoop of Pear Sorbet

Third Course
La Carde de Mamé Antoinette *(see page 187)*
(White Terre de Truffe, Terraventoux)

Fourth Course
Classic Roast Turkey and Stuffing
(La Cavée, Terraventoux)

Cheese Course
Brie Truffé *(see page 186)*, Goat cheese, Banon,
Beaufort, Comté, Roquefort
A Little Green Salad
(La Cavée, Terraventoux)

Dessert
Les Treize Desserts *(see page 190)*
(Coffee and Verbena Tisane)

marquisette

Marquisette is an utterly divine cocktail: refreshing, heady, much more than the sum of its parts. Serve it as an apéritif, alongside olives, cured meats, and tapenade. It is traditionally topped with champagne, though any white sparkling wine will do.

Serves 8–10,

as an apéritif

2 lemons

2 limes

3 x 750 ml bottles of dry white wine

generous ¼ cup (12 oz/60 g) sugar

¼ cup (60 ml) Grand Marnier (or Vin d'Orange, see page 174)

1 bottle of sparkling white wine, to serve

Chop the lemons and limes into ¾ inch (2 cm) pieces and place in a large pot. Pour in the white wine, sugar, and Grand Marnier, then stir to dissolve. Place a lid on the pot and leave to macerate at room temperature for 24 hours.

Once ready to serve, pour the marquisette into a punch bowl. Ladle the mixture into glasses with an ice cube in each, and top up each with a splash of sparkling wine.

vol-au-vents aux fruits de mer

seafood vol-au-vents

Vol-au-vents are delicious little puff pastry pies, traditionally filled with seafood, mushrooms, or chicken in a béchamel sauce. In my estimation, nothing surpasses the seafood version. The sauce is rendered delectable by the addition of the mussel cooking liquor. We make seafood vol-au-vents and a frisée salad with anchovy dressing every Christmas Eve. Serve two to three vol-au-vents per person for a main course. Any leftovers can be refrigerated and reheated in the oven the following day.

Serves 8
(makes 24 vol-au-vents)

For the pastry
approx. 2¼ lb (1 kg) all-butter puff pastry sheets, defrosted in the refrigerator

1 egg, beaten

Equipment: 2 round pastry cutters: 3½ inch (9 cm) and 2½ inch (6 cm) (a pint glass and an egg cup could also do the trick here if you do not own any suitable cutters)

Cont'd overleaf.

Preheat the oven to 425°F (220°C) and line several baking sheets with parchment paper. Remove the puff pastry from the packaging and wait 5 minutes before unrolling. Keeping the parchment paper attached and working quickly so the pastry remains cold, use the large round cutter to cut as many discs as you can from all the sheets. Distribute half of the discs on paper-lined baking sheets . Carefully brush the tops with beaten egg (avoid getting any egg on the sides since this may prevent the pastry from rising). Cut circles into the centers of the other half of the discs using the smaller cutter and remove these inner circles (discarding them or saving for another use) so you are left with rings. Gently place the rings on top of the bases brushed with egg and now brush the tops of the rings as well. Place in the oven and bake for 10–15 minutes, until the shells have risen and are lightly golden. They return for a second bake once filled with seafood so it is acceptable for the shells to still look a little pale in places.

While the first batch of vol-au-vents are in the oven, combine and re-roll the leftover scraps of pastry and repeat the previous steps (apart from the final brush with beaten egg) to make more shells. This second batch of shells must, however, be refrigerated before baking to achieve a good rise: place in the fridge to chill for at least 20 minutes. Once the time is up, brush the tops with beaten egg and bake in the oven for 10–15 minutes, until risen and lightly golden.

You should now have about 24 shells. Store in plastic containers if these have been prepared in advance. If using immediately, hollow the shells by running a knife along the inside of the rings to cut out the puffed inner circles, making sure you don't cut through the base of the shells. Remove these smaller circles with a few layers of pastry below and set them aside to use as lids. The shells are now ready to be filled as directed overleaf (or as you wish).

For the filling

2 lb 14 oz (1.3 kg) mussels in the shell

generous ¾ cup (200 ml) dry white wine

3½ tablespoons (1¾ oz/50 g) butter

6 tablespoons all-purpose flour

scant ½ cup (50–100 ml) milk (optional)

9 oz (250 g) cooked, peeled shrimp

9 scallops, sliced (optional)

1 lb (450 g) boneless, skinless white fish fillet, such as cod, haddock, or monkfish

1 teaspoon freshly ground black pepper

squeeze of lemon juice (optional)

fresh breadcrumbs (optional)

grated Emmental or Cheddar (optional)

Prepare the mussels: place them in a sink filled with fresh water. Pick them up one by one and, using a knife, pull the beard off and scrape away any barnacles growing on the shell. If any are cracked or won't shut when tapped or pressed, discard. Put the prepared mussels in a separate bowl of fresh water as you go.

Pour the white wine into a large saucepan over high heat. Drain the mussels from their water and add them to the pan once the wine is bubbling. Put a lid on and steam, shaking the pan every so often, for 3 minutes, until the mussels have opened. Turn the heat off. Place a colander over a large mixing bowl and pour in the mussels and their cooking liquor. Discard any that haven't opened at all. Set the colander and mixing bowl aside for the shells to cool and for the liquor to settle so any grit or sand sinks to the bottom.

Preheat the oven to 400°F (200°C). Arrange the hollowed vol-au-vent shells on baking sheets and begin the sauce. Melt the butter in a saucepan over medium heat and add the flour. Stirring constantly, cook until the flour smells toasted and you have obtained a paste: this is your roux. Add a ladleful of the mussel cooking liquor, avoiding the fine grit at the bottom of the bowl, and stir to incorporate it into the roux. Continue adding the liquor, ladle by ladle, stirring constantly, until a lovely creamy sauce has formed. The volume of liquid mussels give off varies but you need to end up with approximately 2½ cups (600 ml) of sauce, so top it up with milk if it doesn't look like enough to coat all of the seafood, or conversely, don't add all of the mussel liquor if the desired consistency has been achieved before all of it is used.

Bring the sauce to a simmer and cook for 5–10 minutes, stirring frequently so it doesn't catch. Place a shrimp in each vol-au-vent shell (and a sliced piece of scallop, if using) to ensure there are no arguments at the table. Slice the fish fillet into small chunks. Remove the mussels from their shells.

Taste to check the seasoning of the white sauce. It shouldn't need salt, but the black pepper and some lemon juice can be added (if using). Stir the chopped fish and mussels into the sauce, and mix to coat evenly. Spoon into the vol-au-vent shells on top of the shrimp and cover with the little round lids. If there is filling left but no more shells, place in ramekins and cover with breadcrumbs and grated Emmental or Cheddar.

Bake the vol-au-vents for 20 minutes, then serve hot alongside a frisée salad (see page 156).

les truffes

black truffles

Cousin Anne and her husband, Olivier, grow the truffles for the family Christmas meal with expert help from Cousin Yannick. Black truffles are closely intertwined with our family history. In the nineteenth century, our ancestor Regis Rimbert rented some land that, as luck would have it, was brimming with an unimaginable quantity of black truffles. He picked 30 kilos (70 pounds) a week over a few winters, a quantity that, in a matter of months, enabled him to buy his own land: the fields we continue to work today with vines, olives, and cherries.

We grow our own black truffles to avoid paying an astronomical price: conservatively, $130 per 3½ oz (100 g) at the time of writing. Today, with fewer and fewer annual rainfalls, our truffles are increasingly few and far between, but so far, we seem to be lucky and always have a handful for Christmas Day and a few other celebratory meals at this time of year.

Why include truffle recipes in a cookbook if they are so difficult to grow and expensive to come by? I share these recipes in case you are ever given a black truffle and wonder what on earth to do with it. I'm not suggesting anyone goes out and buys one (unless you are lucky enough to be of substantial means), but it is possible that one day someone might give you one, or it may come in a luxury food basket you've won… If this wonderful event were to happen, here is what we would do with a black truffle in Provence.

Cont'd overleaf.

FOUR RECIPES FOR ONE BLACK TRUFFLE

If the truffle is fresh, it must be cleaned: hold it under cold running water and use a mushroom brush to carefully remove any earth packed into its puckered surface. Dry on a clean dish towel. The truffle is now ready to be sliced and eaten.

TARTINES DE TRUFFES
(Serves 4)

It is my belief that there is no better way to enjoy a black truffle than raw, thinly sliced on toast, sprinkled with new season olive oil and salt. Simply buy the very best baguette you can find and cut off eight ½ inch (1 cm) thick slices (or more, depending on the size of your truffle). Brush both sides of the bread with olive oil, then place on a baking sheet in an oven preheated to 400°F (200°C). Very lightly toast for just a few minutes, turning once—the bread must still be chewy, not crunchy. Remove the slices from the oven and immediately top with the black truffle, very finely sliced. Drizzle over a few drops of olive oil and sprinkle over a pinch of salt flakes. The salt is important. Allow two tartines per person.

BRANDADE DE MORUE AUX TRUFFES
(Serves 8)

Make (or purchase) the classic Brandade de Morue (see page 47). Finely slice the truffle, then quarter the slices and stir into the prepared brandade. Cover and place the brandade in the refrigerator for at least a day to allow the truffle to perfume the whole dish, then spread and serve on freshly toasted baguette for an extra special apéritif nibble. We have this on Christmas Day with Champagne once the whole family has arrived.

PURÉE DE TRUFFES (truffle mash)
(Serves 4)

My great-aunt Tata Edmée likes to put black truffle in luxurious and unbelievably creamy mashed potatoes. Finely slice the truffle, then stir it into 1 cup (250 ml) crème fraîche. Leave in the fridge overnight to perfume. The following day, peel, boil, and mash 1 lb 5 oz (600 g) potatoes. Purée the mash with 4 tablespoons (2 oz/60 g) butter and 3 tablespoons olive oil, and season with salt and black pepper. Stir in the truffled crème fraîche. Tata Edmée serves this quantity of mash as part of a main course to four people with pieces of flaked, poached salt cod on top and a final drizzle of olive oil and some black pepper. It isn't the mountain of mash I am used to, admittedly, but I can see that it would be a shame to lose the truffle in said mountain.

BRIE TRUFFÉ (truffled brie)
(Serves 8)

Buy the best quality brie you can afford. Slice in half, horizontally, as if you were filling it like a cake, and distribute pieces of thinly sliced black truffle on the cut-side of the bottom half. Place the other half of the brie back on top, then wrap it in parchment paper. Leave in a cool room or pantry, but not the fridge, for at least 48 hours to perfume, before serving with the cheese course on Christmas Day or another special occasion.

la carde de Mamé Antoinette

cardoon

Cardoon is a delicious winter/early spring crop from the artichoke family. Although, once prepared, it looks similar to celery, it has a very different taste, similar to artichoke hearts and stems. We eat it on Christmas Day in a delicious white sauce just before the turkey comes. Look for it in farmers' markets.

Serves 6–8

4½ lb (2 kg) cardoon

juice of 1 lemon

3 tablespoons olive oil

2 tablespoons (1 oz/30 g) butter

1 large onion, finely chopped

5 anchovy fillets

2 heaped tablespoons all-purpose flour

5½ oz (150 g) Emmental, grated

1 fresh black truffle, very finely sliced (optional)

salt and freshly ground black pepper

Cut through the base of the cardoon with a sharp knife and separate the stalks. Run the knife along the edges to remove any sharp spikes or leaves. Wash the stalks thoroughly and cut into 1 inch (2.5 cm) chunks, including the hard flesh from the very base of the plant. As you work, place the chunks in a basin filled with cold water and the lemon juice. Work fast, sice the pieces darken quickly once cut.

Drain the chopped cardoon chunks and place in a large pot. Cover with fresh salted water and bring to a boil over high heat. Lower the heat and simmer with the lid on for about 30 minutes, until the cardoon is tender. Poke with a knife to ensure the harder pieces from the base are ready too, and turn off the heat.

Place a colander over a large mixing bowl and drain the cardoon, keeping the cooking liquid, which will be used to make the sauce. Set both liquid and cooked cardoon aside.

Heat the olive oil and butter in a large sauté pan over medium heat. Add the onion and cook, stirring frequently, for 10–15 minutes until soft but not brown. Add the anchovy fillets and squash them with a wooden spatula to help them dissolve.

After 1 minute, sprinkle in the flour and stir well for a further 1 minute. Pour in a ladleful of the cooking liquid and stir. Keep ladling in the cooking liquid as it is absorbed into the sort-of-roux, stirring all the time, until you obtain a simmering thick sauce consistency. You will probably not use all of the cooking liquid.

Stir the cooked pieces of cardoon into the sauce and season with salt and freshly ground black pepper to taste. Continue simmering gently for 10 minutes (or leave to cool and reheat gently when ready to serve). Just before serving, stir in the grated Emmental. Finally, if you are lucky enough to possess one, add the finely sliced black truffle, gently mix, and serve immediately.

les treize desserts

Provence at Christmas: the thirteen desserts

Walk into any Provençal home at Christmas and you will be greeted with a table or sideboard dedicated to piles of oranges, clementines, candied fruit, dates, almonds, and candles: a beautiful banquet scene reminiscent of mystical period feasts, the Provençal *treize desserts*.

Thankfully, for *les treize desserts*, one doesn't have to actually bake thirteen cakes or sweets, there must simply be thirteen dessert options at the Christmas meal: a beautiful plate of mandarins counts as one, a box of Medjool dates as another, and so forth. The number thirteen of course denotes the twelve apostles and Jesus. Elements of *les treize desserts* appear in homes throughout the Christmas period when friends and family drop in to see each other frequently. It means there is always something ready for visitors to help themselves to, and the host or hostess is not constantly preparing things for new guests and arrivals. Each family no doubt has a few variations on the elements of *les treize desserts*, but some things are obligatory.

You will have a bread, either a sweet fougasse or a Pompe à Huile (see page 191), which will be torn, not cut when eaten (I). The four mendicant orders must be represented: the Franciscans, denoted by dried figs, the Carmelites by hazelnuts or walnuts, the Dominicans by almonds, and the Augustinians by raisins. These may be served separately (useful to get the numbers up to thirteen!) or together on chocolate florentines, known, of course, as mendiants (II). Next, a dessert representing the Levant and Bethlehem is customary, usually dates (III).

Then, it becomes a little more relaxed: one can make or buy *oreillettes*, a kind of thin crispy fried cookie (IV), pile fresh fruit in bowls: clementines, oranges, lychees, or kumquats, apples and pears (V, VI, VII, VIII, IX), buy or make sweets, candied fruit, and fruit jellies: quince cheese, nougat, and orangettes (X, XI, XII). Finally, the wildcard: someone (usually my mom) takes it upon themselves to bake something wonderfully kitsch such as a yule log, *la bûche de noël*, a carrot cake iced to look like a snow scene, or a (more traditional) Panade (see page 144) (XIII).

In my family, we save *les treize desserts* for Christmas Day, when the twenty-five or so of us gather to celebrate. The responsibility for providing the different elements is shared.

la pompe à huile

La pompe à huile is a sweet, orange blossom-flavored bread, akin to a brioche in texture, though it is prepared with olive oil and contains no butter or eggs. It is traditionally made using newly pressed olive oil, which at Christmas will be just a few weeks old. I often double the quantities below to make two: one for *les treize desserts* and one for breakfast the day after Christmas, sice it is delicious dunked in hot chocolate… When eating, it must be torn, not sliced.

Serves 6–8

¼ oz (7 g) envelope instant yeast, or ¾ oz (20 g) fresh yeast

3 tablespoons tepid water, plus 4–5 tablespoons for the starter

2¼ cups (10½ oz/300 g) white bread flour, plus extra for dusting

¼ cup (1¾ oz/50 g) sugar

pinch of salt

2–3 tablespoons orange blossom water (according to strength)

scant ½ cup (100 ml) olive oil

First prepare the starter: In a bowl, combine 4–5 tablespoons of tepid water, a scant ½ cup (1¾ oz/50 g) of the flour, and 1 teaspoon of the sugar. Sprinkle (or crumble) the yeast into the bowl, mix well, then cover the bowl with plastic wrap and set aside for 1 hour, until the dough has increased in size and bubbles are visible on its surface: your starter is ready.

Sift the remaining flour into a mixing bowl. Make a well, then add the prepared starter, the 3 tablespoons tepid water, and the remaining sugar, followed by the salt, orange blossom water, and olive oil. Combine, then cover and set aside for 5 minutes for the flour to absorb some of the liquid.

Transfer the dough to a clean, dry, lightly floured surface and begin to knead (a dough scraper or rubber spatula will be useful at this beginning stage while the dough is still likely to stick to your surface). Continuously knead for 15 minutes until a stretchy, springy dough has formed, then shape into a ball and put it back into the mixing bowl. Cover the bowl with plastic wrap and place in a warm, draft-free place to rise. Once the dough has doubled in size, usually after 2–3 hours, punch it down and knead once more for a few moments.

Line a baking pan with parchment paper and place the dough on the paper. Roll into an oval shape, about ½ inch (1 cm) thick. Using a sharp knife, cut three diagonal slits across the dough in the center (but don't go to the edge) and use your fingers to enlarge the openings, then cover with plastic wrap. Leave to proof in a warm place for 1–2 hours. Towards the end of your proofing time, preheat the oven to 400°F (200°C).

Place in the oven and bake for 15–20 minutes, until lightly golden. Remove from the oven and place on a wire rack. Once cool, keep in a bread box until ready to serve.

les mendiants

If making mendiants for an occasion other than a Provençal Christmas, the toppings can, of course, be varied: chopped candied oranges, pistachios, and dried cranberries are beautiful. It is important to use good-quality chocolate otherwise the mendiants will be too thin.

Makes about 40

10½ oz (300 g) dark baking chocolate

⅓ cup (2 oz/60 g) dried figs, quartered, then halved again if large

scant ½ cup (2 oz/60 g) raisins

½ cup (2 oz/60 g) hazelnuts or walnuts, halved

scant ½ cup (2 oz/60 g) almonds

Break up 9 oz (250 g) of the chocolate into small pieces in a heatproof bowl and place over a pan of very gently simmering water, ensuring the base of the bowl does not touch the water. Stirring occasionally, melt the chocolate. Once completely melted, turn off the heat and break in the remaining chocolate. After a few minutes, the additional chocolate should have melted. Take the bowl off the pan and set aside.

Line two baking pans with parchment paper (adding a dot of chocolate to the underside of the paper ensures it doesn't slip). Using a teaspoon, add blobs of chocolate to the lined pans, and then top with the prepared fruit and nuts. Leave to set, at room temperature, then store in a box until Christmas Day.

oreillettes

Delicious little orange blossom-flavored treats: a cross between a cookie and a doughnut.

Serves 10

2 cups (9 oz/250 g) all-purpose flour, plus extra for dusting

2 eggs

4 tablespoons (2 oz/60 g) butter, softened

1 teaspoon baking powder

2 teaspoons orange blossom water

pinch of salt

4¼ cups (1 liter) peanut oil

2–3 tablespoons confectioner's sugar

Sift the flour into a bowl. Add the eggs, butter, baking powder, orange blossom water, and salt. Beat together, then knead for 3 minutes. Cover the dough with plastic wrap and leave to rest in the fridge for at least 2 hours.

Remove the dough from the fridge. On a lightly floured surface, using a lightly floured rolling pin, roll out as thinly as possible. Using a pastry cutter, cut into 2 by 4 inch (5 by 10 cm) rectangles.

Heat the peanut oil in a heavy-bottomed pot over medium–high heat until hot. After about 10 minutes, lower the strips of pastry into the oil using tongs. Continue adding until you have a single layer cooking. Deep-fry for a few minutes, until lightly golden and puffed up. Lift out of the oil using tongs, dab with paper towels, place on a platter, and sprinkle liberally with confectioner's sugar while you fry the next batch. Serve at room temperature. These will keep for a day or two in a cookie jar.

nougat

Papé Xime makes a vast quantity of nougat for the family every Christmas. The nougat mixture must be covered with rice paper on all sides since the mold will be flipped upside down halfway through setting. It's a bit of an art: cook the honey for too long and the nougat will be hard enough to break teeth, cook it for too little time and it won't set. The honey we use is raw lavender honey.

Serves 10

1 tablespoon all-purpose flour, plus extra for dusting

4–6 sheets of edible rice paper

7 cups (2¼ lb/1 kg) whole almonds

3 cups (2¼ lb /1 kg) honey

2 tablespoons sugar

Equipment: 8 by 16 inch (20 by 40 cm) disposable aluminum tray

Preheat the oven to 400°F (200°C).

Prepare the nougat "mold." Lightly dust the aluminum tray with flour, then line with rice paper on the base and sides: use clothespins to clip the rice paper to the sides—these will be removed once the filling is added later. Set aside some rice paper to place on top of the nougat.

Place the almonds on a baking pan and lightly toast in the oven for 5 minutes, then remove from the oven.

Pour the honey into a large saucepan over medium heat and melt, stirring frequently with a wooden spoon. Add the lightly toasted almonds, then, stirring continuously, simmer the almonds in the honey until you hear them whistling and the honey has turned as lovely and brown as the almonds: usually after about 25 minutes.

Stir in the sugar and flour. Mix for 1–2 minutes, then pour the nougat mixture into the prepared mold. Remove the clips, and top with the final piece of rice paper. Weigh the surface down with cans or jars from your pantry.

Let the nougat almost fully set in a cool place for 1 hour, then flip it upside down for 20 minutes, then flip back over. An hour later, while still warm, armed with a large, sharp knife (or a two-handled herb knife) and possibly a mallet, chop into 3 inch (7.5 cm) thick bars, then smaller squares. Nougat keeps for quite some time in an airtight container.

orangettes

Orangettes are absolutely delicious and make wonderful gifts in jars if you can bear to part with some.

Makes approx. 10½ oz (300 g)

4 oranges

5 cups (2¼ lb/1 kg) sugar

5½ oz (150 g) good-quality dark chocolate (optional)

Quarter the oranges and remove the orange flesh so you are just left with the peel and some pith. Slice each peel quarter into ½ inch (1 cm) strips. Place the strips in a pot and cover with plenty of water. Bring to a boil, then simmer for 10 minutes.

Drain away the water, then cover the peel once more with a generous amount (approximately 5 cups/1.2 liters) of fresh water. Bring to a boil again and this time leave the peel to simmer for 30 minutes, keeping an eye on the water level and covering the pot if it seems to be evaporating too fast: this water will be used to make a syrup to candy the peel later, so it is important to have a sufficient quantity.

Drain the slices once more, reserving the cooking water this time, and set aside. Decant the liquid into a measuring cup and note the amount of milileters, if possible: for every 100 ml (scant ½ cup) of liquid leftover, add ½ cup (3½ oz/100 g) of sugar to the pot. There will generally be about 800 ml (about 3⅓ cups) of liquid remaining, as such requiring 4 cups (1 lb 12 oz/800g) of sugar to make a syrup

Put the water back into the pot along with the corresponding amount of sugar over very gentle heat. Stir until the sugar has dissolved, then add the peel. Simmer for 1–1½ hours, until the peel becomes glistening and translucent in places.

Allow the peel to cool in the pot while you heat the oven to its lowest setting and line a baking pan with parchment paper. Drain, then lay the peel, evenly distributed, on the prepared pan, and dry in the oven for 30 minutes. Remove from the oven, sprinkle with plenty of (the remaining) sugar, and toss on the pan with your hands to coat.

Orangettes can be served as they are at this stage, or coated in chocolate. If you wish to make chocolate orangettes, break the chocolate into chunks and melt in a heatproof bowl set over a pan of gently simmering water. Leave the chocolate to cool slightly, then dunk half of each orangette into it. Lay on parchment paper-lined pans at room temperature. Orangettes will keep for a few weeks in jars or sealed in containers.

la pasto de coudon

quince cheese

My mother makes this in vast quantities every year owing to a quince tree orchard her brother Serge owns but has all but given up on… *"Mon champ de cognassiers adoré,"* he will say ironically when we bring it up.

Makes a 10 by 14½ by 2 inch (25 by 37 by 5 cm) dishful

4½ lb (2 kg) quinces

juice of 1 lemon

6½ cups (2 lb 14 oz/1.3 kg) sugar

Equipment:

10 by 14½ by 2 inch (25 by 37 by 5 cm) rectangular oven dish or several smaller dishes

large, heavy-bottomed saucepan

1 person to help you (ideally)

Line the rectangular oven dish with two large sheets of parchment paper overhanging the sides. Set aside.

Wash the quinces but leave them unpeeled. Take a strong knife and quarter each quince, discarding the stems. Gouge out the seed pods and open them carefully to release the seeds. These contain the pectin that will help to set the "cheese."

Place the quince quarters in a large heavy-bottomed saucepan, together with the seeds. Add the lemon juice and cover with cold water. Bring to a boil over high heat, then lower the heat to a simmer and cook for about 30 minutes, until very tender: poke the quinces with a knife to ensure this is the case.

Drain the cooked quinces in a colander and leave to cool. The cooking liquid and seeds can be discarded. When cool enough to handle, peel and discard the rough woody core from each piece of quince.

Return the cooked quince to the rinsed-out pan, stir in the sugar, then purée with a handheld immersion blender. Turn the heat on and bring the puréed quince and sugar to a gentle simmer, stirring regularly. When the first bubbles start to appear, start stirring continually and vigorously with a wooden spoon to prevent splatters, scraping the bottom of the pan as you stir. The hot mixture will tend to bubble up like a geyser so caution is advised. After 30–45 minutes, the quince cheese should be ready: the base of the pan should be visible when a spatula is run through the mixture.

Pour the contents of the pan into the lined dish, fold back the sides of the parchment paper, and add another piece of parchment paper on top, then leave to cool. Keep in the fridge or in a cool place for the jelly to dry and firm up a touch. Once fully set, the cheese can be cut into cubes, wrapped up, and given as gifts. Quince cheese keeps for months.

la couronne des rois

the feast of Epiphany

France celebrates the feast of Epiphany on January 6th with dessert: a galette, gâteau, or couronne des rois to mark the arrival of the three kings to Bethlehem. Each cake is baked with a tiny little porcelain figurine hidden inside, known as the *fève* (a likely eponym since they would have been dried fava beans, fèves in French, in frugal times of yesteryear). As the cake is cut, the youngest person in the room slides under the table and calls out the name of the person who should receive the next slice. She or he that finds the *fève* in their piece of cake becomes king or queen for the day.

In Provence, we opt for a couronne des rois over the famous galette des rois. The lesser known couronne is an orange blossom-flavored brioche, decorated with candied fruit and crunchy pearls of sugar. Its soft, light texture is most welcome after the indulgences of Christmas and one I prefer to the frangipane-filled puff pastry of the galette des rois.

This couronne recipe is my great-aunt Edmée's. She will double or even quadruple the quantities, making multiple cakes at once to give away to friends and family. Is there anything lovelier than gifting someone a homemade cake? I once memorably bicycled home nearly 10 miles (15 km) from her house with a gifted couronne precariously tied to the back of my rickety bike.

Serves 8

For the starter

¼ oz (7 g) envelope instant yeast, or ¾ oz (20 g) fresh yeast

5 tablespoons tepid milk, plus extra for brushing

6 tablespoons all-purpose flour

For the couronne

zest of 1 orange

5 tablespoons sugar

1 tablespoon orange blossom water

2 cups (9 oz/250 g) all-purpose flour, plus extra for dusting

2 eggs, lightly beaten

6 tablespoons (3 oz/80 g) butter, softened

2½ tablespoons chopped candied citrus peel

1 porcelain fève or whole almond

For decoration

3 tablespoons apricot jam

1 teaspoon orange blossom water

8 candied cherries (optional)

8 candied fruit pieces (optional)

2–3 tablespoons pearl sugar

For the starter: Place the tepid milk in a mixing bowl and sprinkle (or crumble) in the yeast. Mix in the flour, then cover with plastic wrap. Leave in a warm place for 1 hour or so, until the dough has risen a little and bubbles have formed: your starter is ready.

For the couronne: Add the orange zest to a large mixing bowl with the sugar and orange blossom water. Mix, then sift in the flour. Add the beaten eggs, softened butter, and prepared starter. Mix with a spoon as much as possible, then take over with your hands. Knead for a few minutes. The dough will be quite sticky.

Transfer the dough to a clean surface sprinkled with flour and continue to knead for 15 minutes. If you find the dough is still very sticky after 5 minutes, add a little extra flour.

Once you have finishing kneading, shape the dough into a ball and place back in the mixing bowl. Cover the bowl tightly with plastic wrap and place in a draft-free warm spot. Leave to rise until it has doubled in size. This will take 2–3 hours in a toasty place.

After a few hours, punch down the risen dough and allow the air to escape. Knead for a minute on a lightly floured surface, then roll into a circle about ¾ inch (2 cm) thick. Transfer to a baking pan lined with parchment paper. Stick a finger in the center to make a hole, then move it around to increase the aperture so that you are left with a shape like a giant, flat bagel, with a hole approximately 2 inches (5 cm) in diameter. Sprinkle the chopped candied peel around the hole and nestle the fève or almond inside it. Fold the outer edges of the dough inwards, over the candied fruit, and press to seal with the inner edge, forming a sort of giant stuffed bagel: your couronne.

Carefully flip the couronne upside down (the bottom side is generally prettier), cover with plastic wrap, and set aside in a warm place to proof for 2 hours. Towards the end of the proofing time, preheat the oven to 400°F (200°C).

When you're ready to bake, remove the plastic wrap and brush the cake with a little milk. Bake for 15–20 minutes, until the top is a lovely deep golden color. Once out of the oven and still warm, the couronne should be decorated. Place the apricot jam in a small saucepan and add the orange blossom water. Gently heat for 1 minute, then brush over the cake to glaze. Top with the candied cherries and candied fruit, if using, followed by a generous sprinkling of pearl sugar. This keeps for 2–3 days in a cake tin.

appendix

CHICKEN STOCK

Many chicken stock recipes require a great many ingredients. I find this unnecessary. The following makes a perfectly lovely stock without sacrificing too many vegetables. If the stock is destined for Asian dishes such as pho or gai tom kha, add a star anise and a cinnamon stick to the mix.

Makes about 8½ cups (2 liters)

1 chicken carcass
1 carrot, peeled and trimmed
1 celery stick (fronds included)
1 onion, peeled and pierced with 2 cloves
2 sprigs of parsley
6 black peppercorns
3 bay leaves

Place all the ingredients in a large stock pot and cover with plenty of water: the carcass should be completely submerged. Cover the pot and slowly bring to a boil. Lower the heat to a simmer, then cook for 1 hour. Strain the stock into a large mixing bowl and leave to cool. Skim any fat from the top, then ladle into pint-size (500 ml) freezer bags. Seal the bags, then freeze until needed. Best used within a few months.

MAYONNAISE

I would encourage readers to get into the habit of making homemade mayonnaise rather than buying it, since it is superior tasting and takes a matter of minutes to make. I whip some up whenever I am making BLTs, roast chicken, coleslaw, or potato wedges.

Makes about 1¼ cups (300 ml)

1 egg yolk
1 heaped teaspoon Dijon mustard
generous ¾ cup (200 ml) neutral oil (peanut or canola)
1 tablespoon olive oil
1 teaspoon red wine vinegar
pinch of salt
pinch of freshly ground black pepper

Whisk the egg yolk and mustard together in a bowl and slowly drizzle in the neutral oil, about 1 teaspoon at a time, whisking continually between each addition. Do not add any more oil until the previous teaspoon has completely emulsified. Once all the neutral oil has been added and a mayonnaise has formed, add the olive oil and vinegar, then season with salt and black pepper.

AÏOLI MAYONNAISE

A garlic mayonnaise: delicious with simple roast chicken, breaded fish, fries, Accras de Morue (see page 101), or Panisses (see page 99). Do not mistake this for a traditional Aïoli (see page 51). This is far more neutral-tasting since it is concocted with a mixture of oils, not just olive oil.

Makes a generous ¾ cup (200 ml)

1 garlic clove, peeled
1 egg yolk
1 heaped teaspoon Dijon mustard
⅔ cup (150 ml) neutral oil (peanut or canola)
3 tablespoons olive oil
1 teaspoon lemon juice
pinch of fine salt

Crush the garlic into a round-bottomed bowl and add the egg yolk and mustard. Whisk together, then slowly drizzle in the neutral oil, then the olive oil, about 1 teaspoon at a time, whisking continually between each addition of oil. Do not add any more oil until the previous teaspoon has completely emulsified. Once all the oil has been added and you have created a lovely mayonnaise, add the lemon juice and season with a pinch of fine salt.

GRAND AÏOLI HELP

Making Aïoli (see page 51) is significantly trickier than mayonnaise since, put simply, olive oil behaves differently to other oils. If your aïoli has "split," that is, gone in seconds from a beautiful mayonnaise to a strange liquid (as has happened to this author many times), do not panic. Take a clean mixing bowl and crack a brand new egg yolk into it. Add 1 heaped tablespoon of Dijon mustard (emergencies are no time to be aïoli purists) and whisk. Next, very slowly, 1 teaspoon at a time, incorporate and whisk the split aïoli mixture into the new bowl until a new mayonnaise is born. It won't be quite as traditional, but you will at least have something lovely to serve your guests.

CROUTONS

Perfect for tossing into salads and soups.

Serves 4

3½–5½ oz (100–150 g) stale bread (baguette or country loaf)
1 tablespoon olive oil
1 heaped tablespoon butter
1–2 garlic cloves, crushed
pinch of salt
pinch of freshly ground black pepper

Cut slices of stale baguette or country loaf into little squares, then place in a dry frying pan over medium heat. Shake the croutons around and toast for 5–10 minutes, until a little golden, then drizzle over the olive oil and add the butter. Add the garlic and continue sautéeing and stirring with caution for a few more minutes, until the croutons are golden brown. Sprinkle with the salt and black pepper.

YOGURT AND CUCUMBER DIP

Delicious with grilled fish or Merguez Koftas (see page 102) as an alternative to the heavier mayonnaise.

Serves 4–6

1 English cucumber (approx. 12 oz/350 g)
2 teaspoons freshly ground black pepper
2 cups (1 lb 2 oz/500 g) plain or Greek yogurt
1 garlic clove, crushed
¼ cup (⅓ oz/10 g) finely chopped mint
¼ cup (⅓ oz/10 g) finely chopped dill
1 tablespoon olive oil
lemon juice
salt

Peel a few strips of skin off the cucumber so it has a striped appearance. Slice the cucumber in half lengthways. Cut each half again lengthways. Chop as finely as you can and place in a bowl. Add the black pepper and yogurt and mix well. Add the garlic and then stir in the fresh herbs, followed by the olive oil. Finally, add lemon juice and salt to taste.

Homemade Red Wine Vinegar

In essence, vinegar is made at home by pouring wine into a vinegar crock and waiting for the resident bacteria to transform it into vinegar. As with bread starters—though don't let this comparison put you off since vinegar requires far less attention—the live bacteria in a crock, known as the "mother," theoretically live and proliferate indefinitely if fed.

Mothers are living heirlooms, the basis for making homemade vinegar forever, to be shared, passed down, and continued through the generations. My mother, Françoise, makes her vinegar from the descendant of a mother that belonged to her parents. I have a vinaigrier (see page 201) with a mother apparently started by my great-uncle Tonton Jo the year I was born. But all traditions, rituals, and mothers have to start somewhere. This is how to begin yours.

La Mère

A vinegar mother is visible: a precious, ideally floating, gelatinous mass called *Acetobacter aceti*. She will make herself at home in your vinegar crock, consuming the alcohol in the wine and transforming it into acetic acid, giving you vinegar in a matter of weeks. Vinegar mothers are drink-specific so one could not, for example, use a cider vinegar mother to make decent red wine vinegar.

Undoubtedly, the fastest way to start making your own vinegar is for someone to give you a piece of their own established mother, made from the kind of alcohol you love to drink and want to use to make your own vinegar. What a gift this is, to give someone the ability to make their own vinegar for life, should they so wish, with a piece of mother coming with her own history, subtly imparting to future vinegars the complexity of the wines that formed her.

To harvest, carefully ladle or snip out a section (at least a tablespoon) of mother from the donor's crock and place her in a jar for transportation. Ensure she is covered with plenty of the vinegar she lived in. Once home, pour her gently into her new crock, add a bottle of wine (if that is the alcohol used), and leave her for a month. If you make vinegar in this way, skip to the Maintenance and Storage paragraph (see page 202).

If you don't know anyone with a piece of mother to give, you must culture your own: a satisfying, joyful task requiring patience. For the purposes of this book, I cultured red wine vinegar mothers, since this is the vinegar I predominantly cook with, however, the method remains the same for white wine or cider vinegar production.

Making your Mother

To culture a red wine vinegar mother, you will need:

– 2 cups (500 ml) Vin-de-Primeur or Nouveau (the current year's wine, for example, Beaujolais Nouveau)
– 2 large, lidless clean jars. (It is sensible to start two mothers simultaneously lest one fails. If you have a 100 percent success rate, give the extra mother away.)
– small glass of unpasteurized red wine vinegar (optional, available from farmers' markets and online)
– 2 pieces of cheesecloth
– 2 rubber bands

The theory goes that the addition of unpasteurized vinegar, likely already containing floating particles of mother, will help a new mother form more rapidly. I have successfully cultured mothers without the addition of vinegar in the same amount of time as those with vinegar, so in my experience this is not an absolutely necessary ingredient.

Pour 1 cup (250 ml) of wine into each jar. Add a splash of the vinegar to each, if using. Cover each with the cheesecloth and secure tightly using the rubber bands: this will keep the air circulating but the fruit flies out. Place the jars in a kitchen cabinet or pantry for 2–3 months.

It is exciting to check on the jars every so often to see what's going on, however, try not to shake or disturb the surface of the wine too much, since this is where your mother is forming, where the liquid meets the air. The contents of the jar will smell like vinegar long before the mother is ready, but you'll know when she is. After a few months, you should detect a red jelly disc floating in your jars. Rejoice! The mother is ready and you can begin making vinegar. But for this she will need a new home, a vinaigrier.

Le Vinaigrier

A vinaigrier is the crock in which the mother will live and the wine will be fermented into vinegar. In truth, I have seen vinegar made in all kinds of containers, but the perfect vessel is a dedicated 8½ cup (2 liter) ceramic crock with a cork tap at the base. You can order reliable ones online if your local cookware store doesn't have one. Additionally, many independent ceramicists have begun to throw them thanks to the recent renewed

interest in home-fermenting. You can also sometimes spot second-hand vinaigriers in vintage markets, which are perfectly useable if the pot is intact, since the wooden taps can be ordered online and replaced if missing or faulty. Soak the taps for a day in water before replacing.

Maintenance and Storage

Place the mother in the crock, then pour in a bottle of wine. Place the lid on the crock and leave for a few months. Resist the temptation to decant any vinegar into a bottle at this stage and get into the habit of pouring any leftover wine (even if just a teaspoon) into the crock or sparing a glass for her whenever possible. Aim to have a half-gallon (2 liters) or more of fermenting wine going at any one time. Once you have a good level of vinegar in the crock, use the tap to decant your first bottle. After a bottle's worth of vinegar has been decanted, the equivalent volume of wine should ideally be added back into the vinegar crock: the better the wine added, the better the resulting vinegar, of course.

Old wine bottles and used corks make good dispensers: cut a small wedge out of the cork, like a tiny slice of cake. Fill the bottle with vinegar, then wedge the cork in the bottle. The vinegar should come out in a dribble. I recommend labeling this bottle, lest it be mistaken for wine by a guest helping themselves in the kitchen.

Your mother will maintain herself as you take vinegar from and add wine to your crock. In reality, "new" mothers are forming and "old" mothers are sinking to the bottom. If your mother becomes very big at any stage, give some layers away or, in the interim, store in sealed jars, submerged in vinegar. Over time, you will produce mature, complex, delicious vinegars: records of the years and the sun that sweetened the grapes that made the wines that made the vinegars.

If you are planning on making vinegar on a larger scale, once the vinegar is ready it can be decanted into bottles, sealed, and stored, or given away as gifts. The same rules apply: always leave a decent amount of vinegar in the crock, and replace the volume of vinegar taken out with wine to keep your mother happy.

index

acknowledgments

Thank you to my wonderful family for all of their help with this book, my mom, Françoise Craig, for help with pretty much everything from start to finish, my dad, Richard Craig, sister Sara Craig, and my youngest sister, Estelle Craig, particularly, for her hard work at the shoot. Thank you to my extended family for lending props, houses, recipes, and for all the love and wonderful meals and harvests together over the years, long may they continue: Anne et Olivier Lieffroy, Edmée et Roland Boudin, Violette Voulan, Dany Chabaud Nollet, Serge Rimbert, and Maxime Rimbert. Thank you also to Ed Griffiths, Alice Hart, Elizabeth Murray, Bobby Holloway, Felicity Cloake, Harry Eastwood, Olivia Walsh, Nathalie Dubant, Josephine Maxwell, John Hamilton, Juliet Annan, Debora Robertson, Jill Norman and the estate of Elizabeth David, and Charlotte Bland. I am very grateful to my editor, Judith Hannam, for her conviction in this book, Rachel Cross, Sarah Kyle, Claire Rogers, Anne Sheasby, and Kitty Coles for their work. Thank you to Susan Bell for taking such beautiful photos. Finally, thank you to Sophie Missing and my agent, Jon Elek.